Also by Krishna Nehru Hutheesing

WITH NO REGRETS

SHADOWS ON THE WALL

GHANDIJI (*for children*)

BRIDE'S BOOK OF BEAUTY (*with Mulk Raj Anand*)

NEHRU'S LETTERS TO HIS SISTER

WE NEHRUS (*with Alden Hatch*)

Dear to Behold

Dear to Behold

An Intimate Portrait of Indira Gandhi

by Krishna Nehru Hutheesing

THE MACMILLAN COMPANY
COLLIER-MACMILLAN LIMITED · *LONDON*

*The Macmillan Company
Collier-Macmillan Canada Ltd.,
Toronto, Ontario*

Printed in the United States of America

Contents

Illustrations

FOLLOWING PAGE 128.

Foreword

IT IS NOW SIX MONTHS since my wife died in London. She was on her way back from the United States, anxious to get home and complete the manuscript of this book. All through the summer of 1967 she had been unwell, but medical checkups gave no indication of heart trouble. I had persuaded her to accept the invitation of her New York publishers to be present at ceremonies connected with the publication of her book *We Nehrus*. I hoped that the change of environment would help restore her health.

As soon as her numerous radio and television broadcasts were over, she wanted to return home, for her heart was set on putting final touches on the present book. I urged her to stay on and have some rest before returning. Maybe it was some premonition of death that made her tell numerous friends in the States that it was her last visit and she would not see them again. She was angry with me for repeatedly asking her to stay on, and at last she wrote to me, "All right, since you don't want to see me home, I will stay on another ten days." Little did I realize what inner urge was pressing her to come home and be with me.

And so she did not come home. In the early morning of November 9, in London, as she was getting ready to go to the airport to fly home, she had a heart attack and died on the spot—alone and with no one to help her. I cannot forgive myself for having insisted on her staying on. If only she had been here at home earlier, as she wanted to be, I would have been at hand to help her and perhaps even save her from this untimely and lonely end. We could at least have been together and bid our last farewell. Instead, I could only hold her cold hand and whisper my love as she lay in her coffin. There was no more the gentle response of her warm hand upon my hand, and the smiling eyes were closed forever.

Krishna had loved her family with an intense love. Her brother, her sister, her niece Indira, and her two sons and husband—that was her world. And as the family was an integral part of the struggle for India's freedom, she also loved her country. After independence I drifted away from the Congress party, because I could not accept all of the Jawahar Nehru policies. That created a problem for her. She was faced with divided loyalties and must often have felt unhappy. Perhaps my opposition and open criticism came in the way of the recognition she richly deserved. As a friend wrote, she was the most outgoing person of all the Nehrus. She was sincere, honest, and devoted, and had the famous Nehru capacity for tireless work.

Years ago, in 1943, I was in prison and she was lonely. On my insistence that she should not take an open active part in the "Quit India" movement, she had remained out of prison to look after our two young sons. Her love for our sons had persuaded her to agree with me. From prison, I suggested that she should take to writing to while away her loneliness. She was a brilliant conversationalist, and her talk sparkled with human-interest anecdotes. For her, "memories were like roses in December," for they brought back the fragrance of the love of her father, who meant so much to her. She was full of life, vivacious, and merry.

I told her that she should just write as if she were talking and later collate all the separate notes she had jotted down and edit them. Thus began her first book, *With No Regrets*, the drafts of which came to me in prison for comments and suggestions. I would return the drafts to her, reminding her of other anecdotes she had narrated to me and suggesting that she include them. *With No Regrets* is a beautiful little book of memories, and it met with immediate success. Jawahar, writing to her from prison, said, "It is a charming book . . . just as you are, sincere, frank, and friendly." An English critic wrote about her: "Deeply patriotic, she displays no element of fanaticism. . . . She never loses her gentleness or her capacity to experience the emotions of anxiety and sorrow."

Since then she has written other books. But she was never as anxious as she was to finish the present book. Indira was one of her deep loves. She adored her and tended to think of her as her own daughter.

As Krishna lay before me, I promised her I would work

on the nearly finished manuscript and fulfill her last wish. She had left behind numerous drafts and odd bits of paper with her jottings. They were in two suitcases containing bundles of papers. All I had to do was to put everything in order and edit the material along the lines suggested in her notes.

In the beginning I was too desolate, but slowly I began her work. Our lovely home since her death has become my mausoleum, where the echo of her voice and cheerful animation reach out to me—following me, guiding me. She seemed to be sitting beside me as I typed her manuscript, and I hope I have not misinterpreted her silent instructions. Once I used to express the old saying "Out of sight, out of mind!" Today I live only with my memories.

RAJA HUTHEESING

Bombay

Dear to Behold

1

Allah's Blessings

THE MARRIAGE of my brother Jawaharlal Nehru and the dazzlingly beautiful sixteen-year-old Kamala Kaul took place in Delhi, the bride's home, in March, 1916. For the hundreds of guests from all over India, elaborate tents had been set up—though "tent" is not quite the word for structures furnished with oriental rugs and a staff of liveried servants. The wedding was an affair of great splendor, and the festivities lasted for ten days. Jawahar and Kamala came to Allahabad to live with us in Anand Bhawan, our many-roomed home that sheltered relatives of three generations.

Their daughter and only child—Indira—was born on November 19, 1917. On that night Anand Bhawan was brightly lit. People were going in and out of rooms. Servants were rushing around to serve soft drinks to the women, Scotch-and-soda to the men. Had Father not been so excited at the prospect of a grandchild—the child of his beloved Jawahar—he would have remembered to celebrate the occasion with champagne, as he did a few days later.

I was ten years old. I knew that Kamala was about to have a baby and that several doctors and nurses were attending her. I wanted to stay close to her room, but my governess, Miss Hooper (we called her Toopie, for I could not pronounce her name), had forbidden it. So I wandered out across the courtyard to the veranda, from where I could see my father pacing up and down; my mother sitting on the divan with Bibi Amma, her elder sister, and other women standing around them—all anxiously waiting for the arrival of the child.

My brother kept aloof, as if to escape from the hubbub of voices. He stood alone, pretending not to be concerned, but now and again his gaze would be fixed on the door behind which his wife was lying in pain, having their child.

It was the custom in India (the custom still continues, though not so strictly) for a young wife to return to her parents' home for her confinement. It was felt that she would be more at ease with her own people than with in-laws, whom she came to know only after her marriage. But Father insisted that his precious daughter-in-law should have her confinement in our home, where he could oversee her care and arrange to have the best doctors and nurses in the country and the most modern medical facilities. So Kamala remained at Anand Bhawan.

After what seemed an age to me, the doctors came out. I rushed across the courtyard just in time to hear the Scottish doctor who delivered Kamala announce to my brother, "It is a bonny lassie, sir."

My mother blurted out, "Oh, but it should have been a boy." She had wanted a son for her only son, and the womenfolk around her pulled long faces in sympathy with her. Father, irritated at her show of disappointment, chided her: "You must not say such a thing, or even think it. Have we made any difference between our son and daughters in their upbringing? Do you not love them equally? This daughter of Jawahar, for all you know, may prove better than a thousand sons." While he stamped away angrily, she nodded silently, somewhat subdued by her husband's reproof.

The baby was named Indira by my father after his mother. My grandmother was a strong-willed woman, exceedingly difficult to oppose, and my father dared not flout her. Jawahar and Kamala wanted the name Priyadarshini for their daughter, which means "dear to the sight" or "dear to behold," and so she was named Indira Priyadarshini. And she is indeed dear to all of us and has endeared herself to all India. I was terribly excited at the advent of the baby. She was tiny but well formed, with enormous eyes and masses of jet-black hair. Our love and affection for each other has grown with understanding and respect as the years have passed by.

Indira was only a few days old when Father proposed a ceremonious visit. She was to be brought into the presence of Munshiji, the majordomo of our big household. Under his charge were our fifty servants, twenty-two horses in our stable, and sixteen or more dogs, some trained as watchdogs and some to the gun for shooting and others just pets. He lived in a cottage in the compound with his wife and son.

This old and trusted employee was held in esteem as a member of our family. To us children, he was an uncle—

gentle and soft-spoken but strict when occasion demanded it. On summer evenings my cousins and I would gather around him and make him tell stories of ancient times when men and women were brave beyond belief. He had an inexhaustible fund of stories, each one exciting, each with a moral of courage, truthfulness, and heroism, which he never failed to impress upon us, and we listened in pin-drop silence.

Some time before Indira was born, he became seriously ill with cancer. Father left no stone unturned to alleviate the disease; he consulted specialists and provided medical care. Every evening on his way home from the High Court he would drop by the cottage, even if only for a few minutes. Mother went several times a day, and so did Kamala.

The doctors had been instructed not to let their patient know the nature of his illness, but he had guessed that it was incurable. On a visit one afternoon Father found him in terrible pain. Seeing Father upset, Munshiji said with a brave smile, "Bhai Saheb [elder brother], do not worry. I am not going to die until I have seen and held Jawaharlal's child in my arms and have given it my blessing. I live only for that day."

And now it was "that day." Indira was wrapped in an exquisite Kashmiri shawl, and the nurse, accompanied by Mother and Bibi Amma, carried her to the cottage. Father arrived at the same time. As the pink-and-white baby was placed in Munshiji's outstretched arms, the grand old man could not control his joy. Tears rolled down his white-bearded face as he looked up at my parents and addressed them with names of endearment:

"Mubarak ho Bhai and Bhabi Saheb. May Allah's blessings go with the child, who should be a worthy heir to Jawahar as Jawahar has proved a worthy and wonderful son to you, and may the child illuminate the name of Nehru."

Though Munshiji had been told that the baby was a girl, he continued to think of it as the grandson of Motilal Nehru.

2

"A Goodly Heritage"

—Psalms xvi:6

WE WERE KASHMIRI BRAHMINS. Our ancestor Raj Kaul (not related to Kamala Kaul's family) came to the court of Moghul Emperor Farruksiar, who was charmed with his learning. Farruksiar presented him with a house in Delhi on the banks of a *nahar* (canal), and our family became known in Delhi as Kaul-Nahar, which was corrupted to Kaul-Nehru. Eventually Kaul was dropped and our name became Nehru.

My great-grandfather Lakshmi Narayan Nehru became the first *vakil* (lawyer) of the East India Company at the court of the last Moghul emperor, but in the Revolt of 1857 his son's family was divested of its property and had to flee from Delhi, along with a multitude of refugees. On their journey to Agra, one of our uncles and his little sister were suddenly surrounded by English soldiers. Kashmiris are often very fair, and the soldiers mistook the little girl to be English and accused our uncle of kidnapping her.

He might have been subjected to hanging, but fortunately his knowledge of English saved the situation.

My grandfather, Ganga Dhar Nehru, who took up residence in Agra, had three sons. Bansi Dhar, the eldest, held judicial posts in the British government of India. His assignment to various localities separated him from family responsibilities. Nand Lal, the second son, was the *Diwan* (chief minister) of Khetri State in Rajasthan when his youngest brother—Motilal—was born.

Motilal Nehru, my father, was born on May 6, 1861. He was a half-orphan at birth, Ganga Dhar having died three months earlier. It was Nand Lal who took over the child's upbringing. My father lived with this much older brother and perhaps got his taste for luxurious living at the court of the raja of Khetri. He was thoroughly spoiled by my grandmother, who doted on him. As a boy he had a violent temper—the famous Nehru temper which we all share.

After ten years in Khetri State, Nand Lal went to Agra to study law and then practiced his profession there at the High Court. When the Court was moved to Allahabad, this ancient city became the home of the Nehru family.

My father went to school in Cawnpore. At college in Allahabad, he tended to be a leader in wild capers, but when he took up the profession of law, he passed his examinations brilliantly. He liked Western ways and Western dress, which was not at all in conformity with the preferences of most Indians. His career began with a three-year apprenticeship in the district courts of Cawnpore, and then he came to Allahabad to practice law at the High Court. Soon after this he married a fair and lovely girl of seventeen, Swarup Rani Thussu.

When his brother Nand Lal died, leaving behind a

widow, five sons, and two daughters, my father undertook their support. His desire to give his nephews and nieces a good home and a good education, as Nand Lal had done for him, spurred him to acquiring financial means. He worked hard, and his practice kept expanding.

In 1889, the year Jawahar was born, Father was a relatively poor man who lived in the heart of the city. In the early 1890's his increased earnings enabled him to move to "Civil Lines," where Europeans and Eurasians lived. Through unremitting attention to his law practice and because of his legal acumen (he was particularly versed in Hindu laws of inheritance, and the Lakhna estate case alone brought him rich rewards), he amassed wealth.

In 1900 my sister, Swarup, was born. (Later she was called Nan, a nickname for Nanhi, meaning "little daughter.") That year father bought a fine old mansion of enormous proportions, built around a central courtyard. He named it Anand Bhawan (House of Happiness) and gave it a masterful renovation to suit his way of living and to make it comfortable for its many occupants.

From the verandas one could look out on a great expanse of garden. Gladioli, daffodils, sweet peas, and roses grew in glorious profusion under the tall jakaranda trees, with their showy clusters of blue blossoms, and the lawns were strewn with bright orange-red blossoms from the flame of the forest trees. Hundreds of birds—parakeets, mynahs, coppersmiths—flitted about, adding their sweet songs and flashing color to the beauty of the garden.

In my childhood, Father had already reached the height of his career, and he spent his large income lavishly. Saving for a rainy day did not interest him at all because, he said, he could earn as much as he wanted whenever he liked. He entertained on a grand scale. His stately drawing room, with the Victorian appointments that were then in vogue, would be filled with men of eminence—Indians as well as foreigners from all over the world—lawyers, artists, sportsmen, and the maharajas who were his clients. The dinner table, set with glittering cut glass, Spode china, fine cutlery, and bowls of gorgeous flowers; the choice wines, suited to the discriminating tastes of his cosmopolitan guests; the serious talk, the gaiety, Father's infectious laughter made our home a center of social life.

Those days Father was so busy heaping success upon success that he had little interest in India's politics. Earlier, in his twenties, he had attended a few meetings of the National Congress but was not much attracted to it.

The National Congress had been founded in 1885 by Allan Hume, an Englishman in the Indian civil service. Later it received the support of Lord Curzon, who became viceroy of India in 1899; he felt that it provided a channel for the expression of political discontent by the Indian people. It appealed to the English-speaking middle class of India, and my father attended meetings as a delegate in 1888 and 1892 and became a committee member in 1902. The Congress, however, did nothing except to meet once a year and pass a few resolutions to draw attention to some grievance and to petition the British government in India. Father took no further interest in the Congress till 1905, when Lord Curzon announced that the province of Bengal was to be partitioned for administrative purposes. The people of Bengal were terribly agitated. A campaign of political terrorism and a boycott of British goods spread to other parts of India. These acts brought about the reunification of Bengal, but unrest continued in the land.

Father, who belonged to the moderate group in the Congress, believed in a constitutional redress of wrongs and strongly opposed the revolutionary actions of the extremists. In a 1907 address before the Provincial Conference of the United Provinces in Allahabad he won adherence to his views. This address made him a target of attack in the extremist press. Even Jawahar, in a letter from England (he was a student at Trinity College, Cambridge), criticized him and called him "immoderately moderate," which made Father very angry. And then Father learned, to his distress, that Munshiji's son, the eighteen-year-old Manzar Ali, had become involved with terrorists. He sent for Manzar and demanded that he mend his ways.

Out of a deep affection and regard for Munshiji, who wanted his son to become a lawyer and compensate for the family fortune lost in the same Revolt of 1857 that had impoverished our ancestors, Father showed him a letter addressed to the wayward son. Munshiji tearfully agreed to it. Father wrote:

Dear Manzar Ali,

I am not quite sure that you have understood correctly my attitude toward you and have therefore made up my mind to write so that there may be no misconception of what I told your father. I suggested that, the college being closed, you should take a holiday out of Allahabad and hence keep out of the influence at work here for a time. I also sent a note to your father saying that it was my wish that you should not attend any political meetings, public or private, so long as you continued to be a student. If you do not care to comply with that wish, you had better take care of yourself, and [I told your father] that Anand Bhawan was not the place for you.

You must understand that if I had one of my own boys to deal with instead of you, I should have acted exactly as I have in similar circumstances. The only possible difference would be that while in the case of these boys I should have been able to nip the mischief in the bud, I was not in your case even aware of your activities. And this simply because you have not been in touch with me of late, though you have lived all this time practically in the same house with me.

I do not expect you to change your views, however widely they may differ from mine, simply to please me. But I have every right to expect that no one living in my house will so conduct himself as to bring discredit on me or my house. I have no wish to discuss the various political propaganda with which the atmosphere at present is thick. Nor is it necessary to enter into the vexed question whether or not students should be prohibited from taking an active part in political movements of the day. I have only to deal with one student and I know that his taking such a part is neither good for himself nor for his country. . . .

Surely you do not imagine that by neglecting your studies and attending political meetings you will bring about the salvation of India within the next eighteen months? I offer you a *locus penetentii* and give you an opportunity to realize the situation. . . . I do not ask you to sacrifice your principles or act contrary to your opinions. I ask you to simply do the first and foremost duty you owe to yourself, your parents, relations, friends, and the country at large. Also to arm yourself for the struggle before you engage in it. Now it is for you to take this opportunity or throw it away. I have done my duty.

Yours affectionately,
Bhaiji

But Manzarbhai (*bhai* means "brother"), a youthful reformer with strong convictions, was determined to liberate India from foreign rule. He rejected Father's counsel and left our home. His departure occurred the year I was born, and I did not know him until long afterward, when he returned as a devout follower of Gandhi, spreading the gospel of nonviolence and civil disobedience from village to village.

Father presided over his household as a benevolent, wise, generous, strict, inflexibly obeyed master. The seven cousins who lived with us were treated just like his own children. They loved him and went to him for advice and guidance. Occasionally I was allowed to play with my boy cousins. We were brought up under rigorous discipline—my brother by an English tutor, Mr. Brooks, and my sister and I by an English governess, Miss Hooper. I was sent off to bed punctually at seven, without the privilege of being present at Father's evening arrival. We did not see enough of our mother either, for her frail health often kept her in her room.

Jawahar's marriage brought a cherished new member into our family. I was then a nine-year-old, too young to think of Kamala as a sister-in-law, nor could she think of me as one. She treated me like a daughter. But Nan and

Kamala were of the same age and behaved as sisters-in-law do—avoiding each other.

The day of Indira's birth was a blissful day for her parents, grandparents, and aunts. Especially for me. Those delightful words of the Scottish doctor, "It is a bonny lassie, sir," were like the sweet sound of village bells. I thought of the child as a little sister. Indira has a heritage of wonderful quality: a father who was handsome and sensitive, an intellectual and an idealist dedicated to a noble cause, a mother of glowing beauty who was tender and brave and a worker in the same noble cause, a grandfather on the paternal side who was a distinguished lawyer, a man of indomitable will and of generosity toward hundreds of people in time of need, and a grandmother who, in spite of physical frailty, did revolutionary work in her old age.

On the maternal side, Indira came from a family of long-established traditions and culture. Her grandfather, Jawaharmul Kaul, was a highly respected businessman in Delhi and exceptionally good-looking, and her grandmother was attractive, sympathetic, and well beloved. My father had taken stock of dozens of Kashmiri families to find the right bride for his son.

3

Mahatma Gandhi Comes to Change Our Lives

WORLD WAR I, proclaimed by the Allied powers as a war "to make the world safe for democracy," came to an end in November, 1918. Shortly afterward, in March, 1919, the British Parliament, forgetting all about the democracy they had espoused elsewhere, passed the Rowlatt Act, which deprived India of the little freedom the country had under British rule. The people were enraged, for the act gave the British rulers "the right to suppress political violence" in India. Arrests without recourse to legal procedures followed. Without warning, the police broke up meetings; they beat up and fired on those who attended them. In the widespread bitter struggle that ensued, Mohandas Karamchand Gandhi emerged as a leader. He was called Mahatma ("great-souled") Gandhi.

Gandhi had returned to India in 1915 after twenty-one years in South Africa, where the mistreatment of the Indian colony in Transvaal and Natal had led him to organize a campaign of nonviolent passive resistance against General Smuts' government. To this movement he gave the namt *Satyagraha*, a Sanskrit word meaning "truth force" or "holding firmly to truth."

During World War I, Gandhi had avoided controversial politics and had even been active in aiding the war by recruitment of an ambulance unit. But in 1919 the passage of the Rowlatt Act aroused his determination to proceed at once against the British policy of repression. He started a *Satyagraha Sabha* (*Sabha* means "an organized association") and appealed to the people to join it. Its members were pledged to disobey unjust laws and to court arrests for civil disobedience.

The newspapers published reports of the program, and it was through the news media that Jawahar first learned of it. The idea of bringing about governmental changes through noncooperation instantly attracted him:

> Here at last was a way out of the tangle, a method of action which was straight and open and possibly effective. I was afire with enthusiasm and wanted to join the *Satyagraha Sabhi* immediately. I hardly thought of the consequences—law-breaking, jail-going, etc.—and if I thought of them I did not care. But suddenly my ardor was damped, and I realized that all was not plain sailing. My father was dead against this new idea. He was not in the habit of being swept away by new proposals; he thought carefully of the consequences before he took any fresh step. And the more he thought of the *Satyagrha Sabha* and its program, the less he liked it.[1]

Father could not believe any good came out of a few people going to jail. The arguments between him and Jawahar put our peaceful home in a turmoil. But Father, ever resourceful, thought up a way out of the predicament: he invited Gandhi to Anand Bhawan. It was Gandhi's first visit to our home. The mutual affection between him and the whole Nehru family began with this visit and continued throughout our lives.

In long talks, Father and Gandhiji (the suffix *ji* is a mark of respect) put forth their respective views on how to arrive at a solution of India's problems. But since Father's original purpose in inviting Gandhi was based on a desire to bring out cogent reasons why Jawahar should refrain from joining the *Satyagraha Sabha*, their exchange of ideas finally centered on Jawahar. To Gandhiji it was apparent that friction between a father and son who loved each other deeply was at stake, and he acquiesced in Father's plea to counsel Jawahar not to make an immediate decision. The counsel turned out to be futile, for fate interposed an event that made a shamble out of all previous arguments. The event was one of indescribable horror—a bloody assault on a throng of unarmed people in Amritsar, a town in Punjab.

From Allahabad, Gandhiji had returned to Delhi to further his movement. There, on March 31, 1919, he proposed a Nationwide *hartal* (nonviolent strike) with the aim of obtaining compliance with the demands for the abolition of the Rowlatt Act. Great crowds came to hear him exhort them to stay away from work. Alarmed by his appeal to the masses, the British authorities arrested him.

Riots broke out in Delhi and other cities. As a consequence, public gatherings were prohibited. This did not deter the irate mobs, who were unaware that Gandhi had been swiftly released. On April 13 thousands of men, women, and children assembled in Amritsar in a place

known as Jallianwalla Bagh, a large open space surrounded by buildings. General Dyer, who had been sent
to disperse the meeting, ordered his battalion of soldiers
to fire on the assembly massed in what was really an en-
closure with only one exit, which he blocked. Hundreds
were killed, and more hundreds wounded. Subsequently,
during a period of martial law, General Dyer heaped
humiliations on those who dared appear in public, such as
barbaric floggings or making them crawl on their bellies
along the street. As a climax to his disgraceful actions, a
group called "The Women of England" raised funds to
present him with a golden "Sword of Honor." However, in
March, 1920, he was forced to resign.

Gandhi, distressed by the riots—for he advocated nonviolence—withdrew his call for *Satyagraha*, but now he
was able to win over the Indian National Congress to his
policy of noncooperation.

Father's reaction to the massacre of unarmed and
peaceful people led to a reversal of his position; he was
now on Jawahar's side, and for Gandhi he had only pro-
found admiration. In a dramatic shift of attitude, he gave
up his lucrative law practice and threw his whole being
into politics. When the Congress undertook an inquiry
into the massacre, Father and Jawahar joined Gandhi as
members of the committee sent to Amritsar to make an
official probe.

The course of events brought a turnabout in the tenor
and direction of our family's way of life. Our table fare,
which was once elaborate with both Indian and Western
cooking, changed to simple Indian food served in *thalis*
(large round platters of silver or of white metal). Each
thali had four to six *katoris* of the same metal, containing

curry, *dal* (mashed lentils), two vegetables, yogurt, pickles, and chutney. With these condiments we had wheat bread, called *chapatis* or *parathas* (baked or fried on a griddle), followed by a serving of rice and a sweet dish for dessert.

The former gay and carefree chitchat was gone. Instead there were heavy political discussions in a solemn atmosphere, except when Father injected a note of lightheartedness and laughter would ring through the house. A stream of guests came and stayed on for days or weeks. Now they were followers of Gandhiji, simply clad in *khadi* (handspun, handwoven cloth). Apart from Gandhiji, who stayed with us whenever he came to Allahabad, our guests included Maulana Mahomed Ali and his brother Shaukat Ali, leaders of the Khilafat movement (it favored the restoration of the caliph), who had joined the Congress; Dr. Ansari, our family doctor and friend; Sardar Vallabhbhai Patel, who was called the "Iron Man of India"; and Maulana Abul Kalam Azad, whose soft and beautiful Urdu speech was interspersed with Urdu and Persian *shere* (couplets). It was a delight to listen to his conversation with Father, who was a Persian scholar. And the poetess Sarojini Naidu charmed everyone with her scintillating wit. Other visitors might just drop in to talk politics —perhaps to plan the next Congress move against the British government in India.

The police swooped down on us at any hour of the day or night—to make an arrest or to cart away costly rugs or furniture in payment of small fines levied on one or another member of the family, who, as a *Satyagrahi*, refused to pay fines. From moment to moment we lived a confused and unpredictable life, never knowing what might happen next. Pilgrimages to prison imposed long separations from loved ones.

The rigid discipline that formerly had regulated the lives of the Nehru children yielded to a permissive freedom. Indira was growing up without orders from a governess. No fixed bedtime for her. A serious, solemn child, she walked around freely to listen with curiosity to grown-ups who were to have a vital role in the history of India. She took in a great deal of what was happening. Father was very proud of his grandchild and made much of her. He showed her off to all visitors.

4

"Joan of Arc"

JAWAHAR HAD RETURNED home from Cambridge in 1912, a time in which political agitation in India had come to a standstill of sorts. However, he brought with him radical views that clashed with Father's moderate views. Their constant conflict disturbed the whole household. But reconciliation was in the offing, partly through membership in the Home Rule League, which Mrs. Annie Besant—the grand old lady of the Theosophical Society—founded in 1916. Jawahar joined the League immediately. One year later the arrest of Mrs. Besant caused Father to join it too. After making an impassioned speech for Home Rule, he was elected president of the Allahabad branch. He had begun to abhor the fawning appeals to the foreign rulers who treated the Indians with contempt.

It was the Defence of India Act—a repressive measure passed during World War I for the undeclared purpose of enrolling recruits in India—that provided the British with justification for Mrs. Besant's arrest. But she was soon released, for the British had a political trick of alternately arresting and releasing the leaders of India. The arrest occurred in June, 1917, and in August the British government issued a declaration of policy of seemingly conciliatory aim—namely, the "progressive realization of responsible government in India as an integral part of the British Empire."

The Indian people faintly expected that the new policy might assure civil liberty, but the lack of progress toward Indian participation in the administration of their country portended nonfulfillment of such expectations. Abruptly, in 1919, the passage of the Rowlatt Act (see Chapter 3) crushed all hopes. It shook Father loose from his faith in constitutional reform—a faith based on his legal background. Now there could be no respect for the rule of law.

In the autumn of 1920 the Indian National Congress, meeting in a special session, passed a resolution accepting Gandhi's policy of noncooperation. The program drawn up included the boycott of titles, of government-owned or -aided schools and colleges, of law courts, of legislatures, and of foreign goods. It declared for resistance to unjust laws and willingness to suffer imprisonment peacefully. Thus Gandhi's policy of *Satyagraha* became the Congress policy.

With the abandonment of his law practice, father had put an end to big earnings, and we had to learn to live in a simple style. The large number of servants was reduced to a few. The Spode china and Venetian glass, the stock of choice wines, and our prized horses and dogs were sold. Luckily, Mother and Kamala had a collection of jewelry that represented a store of wealth—rings, earrings, necklaces, bracelets, and brooches of gold, studded with diamonds, emeralds, rubies, and pearls. Except for a few pieces, Mother and Kamala consented to selling their gems.

Father made a gift of our home to the Indian National Congress. We remained there for several years while a smaller house was under construction. Father's plans for the "smaller" house began with the idea of functional simplicity, but when we moved in, in 1929, it wasn't simple at all. It was a beautiful house, which I have dearly loved. Our new home was again named Anand Bhawan, and the gift to the Congress was named Swaraj Bhawan (House of Independence).

At first I resented having to wear the coarse, handspun, handwoven *khadi*, but after a while it seemed the common-sense thing to do. Somehow the new mode of life, with its austerities, cast a spell over us.

But we were to have one more grand affair—a wedding. On May 10, 1921, Swarup and Ranjit Sitaram Pandit, a Brahmin barrister-at-law and Sanskrit scholar, were married in the presence of both their families, Gandhiji, and many Congress members. The bride wore a *khadi* sari finely spun by Gandhi's wife. My father saw to it that the wedding festivities were as brilliant as possible under the circumstances, with police on the alert nearby.

The groom's family conferred a new name on Swarup—Vijaya Lakshmi. From that time on she was known as Vijaya Lakshmi Pandit.

Mother doted on Indira, and Jawahar's scolding her for an excessive show of affection had no effect. Indira called her Dol Amma and not Dadi, the proper word for grandmother. *Dol* is a shortened form of *doli*, which means a cupboard with metal netting. Mother kept all sorts of sweets in her *doli*, and she fed Indira forbidden tidbits between meals. That's how she got the name Dol Amma.

The atmosphere of politics that pervaded our home put unusual ideas into Indira's head. Growing up almost alone, she amused herself by playing political theater, using dolls for dramatic scenes. She dressed them in fineries or simple peasant garments and arranged them on a table in formation, faced by tin policemen with *lathis* (long, weighted sticks) and tin soldiers with guns. She put Congress flags of paper into the hands of dolls and then lectured the assemblage, for she had seen Gandhi and her grandfather and father in this role. Calling upon her *Satyagrahis* to march forward and keep the Congress flag flying, she asked them not to fear the might of the British government. From the high walls of Anand Bhawan she had watched similar processions of Congress volunteers clad in white *khadi* and carrying the Congress flag aloft.

Indira was also fascinated by the bonfires of foreign clothes—her father's and grandfather's Saville Row suits, ties, shirts, hats—for Gandhiji had called for the boycott of foreign goods. Kamala's and mother's beautiful silk saris and brocades were also heaped on the fire, to accord with Gandhi's advocacy of a life of abstinence and the revival of simple homespun clothes. Little Indira decided that this was the right thing to do. Her daily life was inseparable from the national struggle for freedom. The spirit of the times was described by Jawahar: "Many of us who worked for the Congress program lived in a kind of intoxication during the year 1921. We were full of excitement and optimism and a buoyant enthusiasm."[1]

But soon Jawahar was to spend more time in prison than at home. Indira's earliest memories are of cruel separation, as one or another member of the family was suddenly hauled to prison. She was lonely in a big house that seemed empty to her. Having no governess to chide her, she would go to her grandmother to ask for sweets or to her grandfather to ply him with questions, which he always answered no matter how busy he was. When her father came home from jail, she would hold his hand and ask him to give reasons for all that had happened.

Perhaps it was her grandfather who influenced her more than anyone else in her childhood. Many years later she was to give evidence of her esteem and affection for him:

> I admired my grandfather as a strong person, and I loved his tremendous zest for life, which he had and which my father also developed later on; but I was tremendously impressed with my grandfather's bigness—I don't mean physically—but, you know, he seemed to embrace the whole world. I loved the way he laughed.[2]

Motilal Nehru looked like a Roman senator in his white *kurta* (knee-length shirt) and *dhoti* (long loincloth), with a white shawl thrown across his shoulders—all in the prescribed *khadi* cloth. He wore a white *khadi* cap, which became the symbol of a congressman. His impressive appearance was noted by a newspaper reporter, Sant Nihal

Singh: "The homespun in which he was clad was coarse. It seemed to add distinction to his handsome face and figure."

Jawahar carried a message of hope to the hungry and poor of India. He traveled from village to village talking to the peasants, encouraging them to work for the independence of India and for a better life. His activities aroused British fears, and his arrest was imminent. Henceforward Indira's life was to be one of cruel separations from her family, often with her left alone in the big house.

On December 6, 1921, Indira, at the age of four, had her first baptism of fire when the police entered Anand Bhawan to arrest Father and Jawahar on the charge of being members of the Congress Volunteer Corps and of distributing leaflets calling for the boycott of British goods. The trial was held the following day. Indira sat on her grandfather's knees as he refused to recognize the court or to offer any defense as a *Satyagrahi*. The farcical trial ended with the court's sentencing Father to six months imprisonment and a fine of five hundred rupees. Indira sat quietly, trying to fight back uncontrollable tears. Jawahar got the same sentence.

We returned to our empty home, which seemed lifeless. The next day the police came again—this time to confiscate some of our priceless carpets. Silently but with boiling anger, we watched them take away things of great value in compensation for the nonpayment of fines imposed on Father and Jawahar. Little Indira, however, stamped her feet and shouted, "You can't take them, they belong to us." She flew at the police inspector, shaking her fists at him. We had to pull her away and calm her.

Soon after the arrest, those of us who were still free went to Gandhiji's *ashram* (hermitage or retreat) at the town of Sabarmati in Gujarat near the textile town of Ahmedabad, taking Indira with us. The annual Congress session was being held there, and Gandhiji wanted us to attend it and stay with him. Life at the *ashram* was austere: eating plain, dull, salt-free food, cleaning up, washing floors, sleeping on the floor, getting up at 4 A.M. and assembling for prayers on the banks of the Sabarmati River. We, who were used to luxuries, were taken aback in the beginning but soon got used to the austerities as a foretaste of the life of a *Satyagrahi* in the service of the Congress. Only mother, who was very frail, and the wife of a cousin of ours, Uma Nehru, were exempted from the daily chores. All guests and all who lived at the *ashram* had to assemble in the early cold gray light of the dawn for the prayers, which included readings from Hindu scriptures, the Koran, the Bible, and other religious books and the singing of hymns and devotional Indian songs. I loved these prayers. Young Indira took everything in stride as a novel experience and enjoyed it. She became very dear to Gandhiji, who loved little children.

We returned from Sabarmati to a home bereft of its former splendor. In the absence of father and Jawahar, we womenfolk threw ourselves into political work, attending meetings and joining Congress processions. Kamala and I took to wearing a *khadi kurta,* pajamas, and a Gandhi cap. Indira insisted on having similar clothes, for she thought of herself as a Congress Volunteer. Though she spent most of her time at home with her grandmother and her great-aunt Bibi Amma, she was well aware, from all the political discussions she had heard, that it was our duty to be devoted to the ideal of freedom for the Indian people. In a sense she had no childhood, nor did she have playmates. The few children among our relatives were kept away by their parents, who were afraid of our politics.

Indira was very thin, and her health was a source of worry to Jawahar. His letters from the Lucknow prison in 1922 (his second imprisonment) told of his deep love for his daughter and how he ached to be with her. "Tomorrow it will be three months since I saw her," he wrote, "and she was very pale and weak. I wish some arrangements could be made for her lessons. I am confident that I could have managed her easily—but I am in Barrack 4." To Indira he wrote:

> Love from Papu. You must get well quickly, learn to write letters, and come and see me in jail. I am longing to see you. Have you plied the new spinning wheel which Dadu [her grandfather] brought for you? Send me some of your yarn. Do you join Mother in prayers every day?

Then again,

> Love to dear daughter Indira from Papu. Did you like Calcutta? Is it better than Bombay? Did you see the Calcutta Zoo? What animals did you see? Have you seen a huge tree there? You must get strong and plump before you return to Allahabad.

Indira attended so many different schools that it is difficult to recall them all. When she was six years old, Father (after consulting Kamala) arranged for her to be enrolled in the St. Cecilia High School in Allahabad, where I had been a student for a short while after my governess got

married. It was run by three English sisters, the Misses
Cameron, and was coeducational even at that time. The
selection of an English school led to all sorts of rumors—
namely, that my brother, who had recently come out of
prison, was not happy about it, that it had induced quarrels between him and Father, and so on. These reports
reached Gandhiji, who wrote to Father pleading for
Jawahar's cause. Father's reply, by way of a telegram,
labeled the story as a "tissue of lies, too mean for the
proudest father in the world." He informed Gandhiji that
Jawahar's objection was based not on the principle of noncooperation with foreign institutions but on his doubts
about the quality of education at St. Cecilia. Father had
been prompted by a desire to give Indira the companionship of children of her age, and to this Jawahar had
agreed. Many years later, in the middle of the Quit India
movement, my sister sent her three daughters to the
United States for their education, which again produced
criticism. I relayed this news to my brother in Ahmed-
nagar Fort prison. He replied that my sister's decision was
right.

But our political and unsettled life precluded a regular
school education for Indira. Perhaps the love of books all
of us had and the well-stocked library at Anand Bhawan
was as good a school as any. Over the years we sent books
to each other as presents. From his prison cell Jawahar
would periodically order a number of books for Indira,
and she would read fairy tales, children's editions of
Shakespeare, Dickens, Shaw, and many of the classics that
had been bought for me. Today they are in the children's
library at Teen Murti House in Delhi, which was Jawahar's residence as Prime Minister and is now a memorial to him.

In reading one book after another, Indira had her favorites. She was fascinated by stories about Joan of Arc. One day I saw her standing at the balustrade of the veranda with outstretched arms—one hand pressed resolutely against a stone column, the other hand raised high as if persuading an audience of her mission—an occasion I first described in *We Nehrus:*

> She seemed to be muttering something, so I went up to her and asked, "What in the world are you trying to do?"
>
> She looked at me solemnly with her round little face ringed by jet-black hair and her dark eyes burning, and said, "I'm practicing being Joan of Arc. I have just been reading about her, and some day I am going to lead my people to freedom just as Joan of Arc did."[3]

And so, acting out a story she had read, she felt that she was taking part in her country's call to the struggle for freedom. Later she was to respond to the call with complete dedication.

"Proud of Our Womenfolk"

AFTER INDIRA'S BIRTH, Kamala showed signs of a weak constitution; she tired easily, and her convalescence extended over many months. In 1924 she gave birth to a son who lived only three days. Again, her recovery was very slow, requiring a long period of hospitalization. The healthy girl Father had chosen for his son became chronically ill. Eventually diagnoses revealed that she had tuberculosis. For her tubercular condition the doctors recommended treatment in Switzerland.

So, early in March, 1926, Kamala and Jawahar sailed for Europe, taking their daughter with them. Father planned to go a little later, and I was to accompany him. He needed a rest, but unfortunately a case he had handled many years earlier came up in May for adjudication, and he had to postpone his trip. He insisted on my going as planned, because I had never been abroad and because I could be of help to Jawahar in looking after Kamala and managing the apartment they had taken in Geneva. Besides, he wanted me to enroll in the International School in Geneva and learn some languages, since I had been denied a formal education due to our involvement in politics. Mother was aghast at my traveling alone and wanted me to get engaged to a Kashmiri boy before I left.

I sailed for Europe in June. Jawahar met me at Naples and from there we went to Geneva. He had decided that Indira should attend a school regularly and had placed her in the École Nouvelle at Bex in the mountains. Having grown up surrounded by adults, in a tense political atmosphere, Indira had different interests from other children of her age, for she was far more mature. She knew what the struggle for political freedom meant and had at least an inkling of politics in Europe. Her schoolmates seemed to be solely interested in games and not at all in politics. Indira had no desire to participate in their activities, and she kept aloof from them. Fortunately, like her father and me, she loved winter sports. After many a nasty toss, she learned to ski and skate and loved it.

In the apartment, I was learning the mysteries of housekeeping with the help of our maid Marguerite, who also taught me to speak French. I entered the International Summer School, where distinguished speakers from various countries—statesmen, artists, scientists, writers, and learned men and women from different spheres of life—instructed the students through fascinating lectures.

As Kamala's health had not improved satisfactorily, we moved to another Swiss resort, which had an excellent sanatorium at Montana-Vermala. With Kamala under proper care, Jawahar and I took trips to the cities and villages of Italy. Whenever Kamala was well enough, she and Indira would accompany us.

We visited Romain Rolland, who was living at Villeneuve, not far from Geneva. Indira, with the air of gravity of an old judge, listened to the ideas exchanged between her father and this gifted man of letters. The talk was much too deep for a nine-year-old girl, but my brother believed that her being intimately associated with eminent men and women would do her good. He wanted to expand her outlook, in preparation for the kind of role in India's national life that all of us assumed as a patriotic duty. She seemed to hunger for knowledge and was always very attentive to the conversations. In Geneva she met the German poet and dramatist Ernst Toller and also many Indian exiles—the old revolutionaries, who talked ardently for nationalism. Such contacts furthered her education.

In the summer of 1927, Father came to Europe, and it was wonderful for all of us to be together. We missed Mother, but she preferred to stay at home. Kamala was feeling much better, and so we traveled quite a bit. Father took us to London, Paris, villages and cities of Switzerland, and to Berlin. Unlike Jawahar, he insisted on first-class luxurious accommodations.

While in Berlin, we received an invitation from Moscow to attend the Tenth Anniversary celebration of the October Revolution. We overcame Father's disinclination to go, and he finally agreed. Indira went back to her school, for he thought that the ceremonious events would be a strain on her health. Besides, a child would not be welcome at formal functions.

The Soviet celebrations had a spectacular quality, and the state banquet in honor of the guests of the Soviet government was a magnificent affair. The Russian hosts seated at our table charmed us—in English and French. We saw much of Moscow, and we thought that the faces of people on the streets showed a peaceful contentment with the changes that had come to their country. Our visit lasted a week.

Kamala and I were somewhat bewildered when we found that our mentor, Suhashini (she was the sister of our close friend and Congress leader Sarojini Naidu), had given us very bad advice when we were still in Berlin. This avowed and highly emotional Communist had informed us that the proper clothes for us to take to Moscow were plain *khadi* saris, which we did. To our surprise, she appeared at the festivities in Madrasi silk saris of gay color. When I chided her, she made a scornful reply: "Why, kid, for us Communists it is the right thing to do. You bourgeois must come in sackcloth."

To Father the new Russia seemed drab and ugly, but Jawahar was excited at seeing a communist state. In his autobiography, written fourteen years later, he commented on his being drawn to socialism and communism:

Russia apart, the theory and philosophy of Marxism lightened up many a dark corner of my mind. History came to have a new meaning for me. The Marxist interpretation threw a flood of light on it, and it became an unfolding drama with some order and purpose, howsoever unconscious, behind it. In spite of the appalling waste and misery of the past and the present, the future was bright with hope, though many dangers intervened. It was the essential

freedom from dogma and the scientific outlook of
Marxism that appealed to me.[1]

We had a few more days in Berlin and Paris, and then
Kamala, Jawahar, Indira, and I went to Marseilles to
catch our ship for the homeward journey. (Father stayed
on a little longer to tour more of Europe.) We landed in
Colombo in December, 1927, and went straight to
Madras, where the annual Congress session was being
held. There seemed to be an upsurge of activity in the
whole country—a renewed fervor for dedication to the
principle of freedom.

The contacts in Europe with intellectual socialists had
had a stimulating effect on Jawahar. Spurred by idealism,
he had launched out on his campaign for independence.
He found a ready response at the Madras Congress, and
his resolutions on complete national independence and
anti-imperialism were passed with great enthusiasm by
the youth who had flocked into the Congress. Gandhiji,
however, was unhappy and wrote to Jawahar. "You are
going too fast. You should have taken time to think and
get acclimatized."[2]

In February, 1928, the British sent the Simon Commission to Delhi, vested with authority to grant changes in
India's constitution. It was boycotted. The December session of Congress was held in Calcutta, and Father was
again elected president. But he and Jawahar had come to
a point of dissension. Father espoused moderation and
Dominion status, while Jawahar struck out for full independence. They quarreled briefly. Then a silence fell between them; but publicly, from the platform of the Congress, they attacked each other's views. Ultimately a

compromise resolution was proposed by Gandhiji and accepted. The British government was called upon to grant Dominion status to India within one year; if it failed to do so, the Congress would then work for complete independence from the British.

In October, 1929, the viceroy, Lord Irwin, made an announcement about a projected Round Table Conference in London on the subject of possible Dominion status for India. Immediately a group of Indian leaders, doubtful about any good coming out of a British-led conference, formed a Leaders' Conference of their own (both Gandhi and Father attended it). They issued a manifesto affirming that if full Dominion status were granted within one year and if certain other conditions were met, India would discontinue its policy of noncooperation with the British government.

The discussion proposed by Lord Irwin took place in Delhi:

> Father was there, and Bhai ["brother," our name for Jawahar] went too, though unwillingly. Gandhiji went, of course, for, without him, there would have been nothing. There were representatives of other Indian points of view. All parties finally agreed on a formula envisaging Dominion status as the basis of the conference. Except for Subhas Bose, they all signed the agreement—Bhai only after strong persuasion from Father and much heart-searching. "A bitter pill," he called it.
>
> The agreement never had a chance. Such an uproar now broke out in England that the government had to backwater. Indian opinion was infuriated by the imperialistic speeches of such Conservative lead-

ers as Birkenhead, Winston Churchill, and Lloyd George.[3]

Various Congress committees had met in the summer and autumn of 1929 to deliberate on possible presidential candidates. Gandhi was their choice, but he declined; instead, he urged the members to elect Jawahar. At the December session, held at Lahore, Father proudly handed over the reins of the Congress to his son. Jawahar found a ready response to his ideas among the enthusiastic youths who had joined the Congress. A resolution in favor of independence was passed.

New Year's Day, 1930, was a glorious and memorable day—both for our family and for the vast multitude gathered on the banks of the Ravi River to hear Jawahar deliver his declaration of independence. Indira, dressed in the Congress Volunteers uniform, was ecstatic. She had sat by her father's side when he drafted the document, and she had read it aloud to him. Now she listened intently as her father inspired his audience with these solemn and passionately patriotic words:

> We believe that it is the inalienable right of the Indian people, as of any other prople, to have freedom and to enjoy the fruits of their toil and have the necessities of life. . . . We believe also that if any government deprives a people of these rights and oppresses them, the people have a further right to alter it or to abolish it. The British government in India has not only deprived the Indian people of their freedom but has based itself on the exploitation of the masses, and has ruined India economically, politically, culturally, and spiritually. We believe, therefore, that India must sever the British connec-

tion and attain *Purna Swaraj*, or complete independence....

We hold it to be a crime against man and God to submit any longer to a rule that has caused this fourfold disaster to our country. We recognize, however, that the most effective way of gaining our freedom is not through violence. We will therefore prepare ourselves by withdrawing, so far as we can, all voluntary association from the British government, and will prepare for civil disobedience, including nonpayment of taxes. . . . We therefore hereby solemnly resolve to carry out the Congress instructions issued from time to time for the purpose of establishing *Purna Swaraj*.[4]

The Indian National Congress adopted Jawahar's declaration as the nation's goal. To commemorate the adoption, it set January 26 as Independence Day. On that day the Congress took the pledge for independence.

Gandhiji called on the people to offer *Satyagraha*—this time in a wholly new form. He asked them to break the salt laws. The state salt monopoly prohibited the collection of salt from seawater. On March 12, 1930, he began a march on foot to Dandi, a small seacoast village about two hundred miles from Ahmedabad, where he was to break the laws. Thousands joined him on the way. On their arrival at Dandi in early April, they spent the night in prayer. In the morning, Gandhi entered the sea to collect water, from which he then extracted salt. Throughout the country, people began to make salt in evaporation pans.

At first Father and Jawahar considered this gesture of defiance to be of little consequence, but the movement

became the symbol of freedom, and all of us joined it. In
the words of Jawahar,

> Today the pilgrim marches onward on his long
> trek. The fire of a great resolve is in him and sur-
> passing love of his countrymen. And love of truth
> that scorches, and love of freedom that inspires. And
> none that passes him can escape the spell, and men
> of common clay feel the spark of life.[5]

The British characterized the move as childish, but
they soon came to see incipient dangers in the extensive
involvement of the whole people. They inflicted another
ruthless repression on India. Ordinances were passed to
disperse peaceful processions. The police were given
orders to flog the people with *lathis* and to fire on them.
The savage attacks aroused a fury in the masses of India
—men, women, and children—and a courageous determination to defy the British.

Thousands of people, including Gandhi, Father, and
Jawahar, were arrested. It was up to Kamala, Nan, and
me to take over as much of their work as possible. We
conducted meetings and carried out Congress directives.
My old delicate mother took up picketing, led processions, and faced a *lathi* charge. Kamala, unmindful of her
health, rushed about the city and the whole district (she
was president of the Allahabad District Congress) in
furtherance of the civil disobedience movement. Her
strenuous activities and high spirits had a heroic quality.

Indian mythology and history are full of women warriors, saints, and goddesses. Among these formidable
women were the Rani of Jhansi, who fought against the

British only a hundred years ago, Queen Didda of Kashmir, who fought the Moghul invaders, and many other warrior queens who led their armies into battle. There were also famous mathematicians, like Lilavati, who sat beside her brother, King Harsha of Kanauj, as an equal, and there was the saint Mirabhai, whose songs are sung all over India even to this day. Our scriptures tell of Hindu deities like Shiva, Krishna, and Rama, whose names are always coupled with the names of their spouses; thus the prayers are offered to Shiva Parvati, Radha Krishna, Sita Rama, and not just to the male deities. Our religion has recognized the unity of man and woman in the concept of Ardhanareshwar—a deity half man, half woman. No religious ceremony could be performed without the participant's wife sitting beside her husband.

Gandhiji appealed to the women of India to take their rightful place beside the men. He stressed that freedom could not be won by men alone. Women—half of humanity—must come out of their enforced seclusion, stand shoulder to shoulder with men, and play their part equally in the struggle. His appeal struck a ready response. Women came forward to help the men—at first, in 1921, only a few, but by 1930 in large numbers. They walked in processions, faced the police *lathis* and bullets, and courted the hard life of prison. They stood in the hot summer sun, picketing foreign cloth and liquor shops. They became presidents of Congress organizations and carried out the day-to-day tasks in their areas.

I was secretary of the Youth League and had the honor of being the first to be arrested on the distaff side of our family. Indira, feeling left out, applied for work as a volunteer. But she was only twelve, too young for enrollment. Determined to have a role in Congress activities, she decided to do things on her own.

She rallied the children of the neighborhood—boys and girls, rich and poor—and asked them to bring all the children they could collect to our back lawn for a meeting, at which she would expose a thrilling plan. The next day our lawn teemed with several hundred youngsters. Indira addressed them like a veteran speaker. Her proposal: to set up a children's volunteer organization to work for the Congress, which, she said, was fighting for the freedom of the country. They were to be of use to the Congress in mysterious ways that she had devised.

"No doubt there is risk," she said, "in doing what I am suggesting. If we are caught by the police, we will probably not be sent to prison like the grown-ups, but we might be punished in some other manner and might even be whipped." She asked if they were prepared to serve the motherland. For the assembled boys and girls it was a call to arms. Conscious of what was happening around them, how their parents were facing *lathi* charges and bullets, they agreed unanimously. The element of danger was itself an attraction, for they had yearned to be involved in the exciting risks faced by their elders.

Indira named her organization *Vanar Sena* (Monkey Army), after a story in the old Hindu epic Ramayana. King Dasaratha of Ajodhya had three wives by whom he had three sons: Rama, the eldest and heir apparent, Lakshmana, and Bharat. The mother of Bharat was a crafty woman who aspired to have her son succeed to the throne. Having succeeded in extracting a promise from

Dasaratha to grant her a wish, she asked that Rama be sent into exile with his wife Sita. Lakshmana loved his brother Rama and followed him into exile. One day, while they were hunting in a forest, the demon king of Lanka, Ravana, who had fallen in love with the beauty of Sita, came to their hut and abducted her. The brothers looked everywhere but found no traces of her. Then Hanuman, the king of the Monkeys, appeared to tell them that his followers had seen Ravana take Sita away, and he offered to go on a search for her. Hanuman found her in a beautiful garden in Lanka, sitting under a tree and weeping. He jumped down from the tree he had climbed and told her to have courage, for Rama would soon come and rescue her. When Rama and Lakshmana heard where Sita was, they did not know what to do. Their army was inadequate to fight the powerful Ravana; besides, they had to cross the sea to go to Lanka. Hanuman again offered his help, collected his tribe of monkeys, and joined Rama's army. They built a bridge by throwing huge rocks into the sea, defeated Ravana, and rescued Sita.

Indira adapted the story to practical purposes. The bridge she built was a bond of union between children and adults. Thousands joined her Monkey Army. She drilled them, marched them, and instructed them in their allotted duties. They worked as an auxiliary to the Congress—making flags, addressing envelopes, serving water to the volunteers in processions. The more daring youngsters went around sticking up notices of meetings and processions when it was dark. They bravely carried messages from one group to another in a truly underground system. Seemingly innocent, they ran in and out of houses surrounded by police about to make an arrest. The police ignored them, thinking they were just a bunch of inquisitive youngsters who merely wanted to see what was happening. Little did they guess that the children were delivering important instructions from the Congress that they had learned by heart.

In later years Indira was often questioned about this adventurous heroic feat. She gave the reasons for its success in these words:

> Nobody bothered about an urchin hopping in and out of the police lines. Nobody thought that he could be doing anything. Well, the boy would memorize the message and go to the people concerned and say: "You know, this is what has to be done, or not done. All the police are there. So-and-So is going to be arrested," or whatever the news was.
>
> In a similar way, we also acted as an intelligence group, because frequently the policemen, sitting in front of the police station, would talk about what was going on—who was to be arrested, where there would be a raid, and so on. And four or five children playing hopscotch outside would attract no one's attention. And they would deliver this news to the people in the movement.[6]

The independence movement went on gaining strength, which, of course, provoked more and more arrests. Father and Jawahar were in Naini prison. The Congress Working Committee had been declared unlawful. As its leaders were arrested, they appointed others to the committee, who were arrested in their turn. In this way several women, including Kamala, had become members of the Working Committee. In the new India that was emerging, women were taking their rightful place, welcomed by men to share in the tasks that lay ahead. Jawahar, in his autobiography, expressed his gratefulness for the work being done by women:

> We felt proud of our people and especially of our womenfolk, all over the country. I had a special feeling of satisfaction because of the activities of my mother, wife, and sisters, as well as many girl cousins and friends. . . . We grew nearer to each other, bound by a new sense of comradeship in a great cause. The family seemed to merge into a larger group, and yet to retain its old flavor and intimacy.[7]

And so all members of our family, young and old, were doing their bit for the cause. The grapevine carried the news of our activities to Father in prison, and he wrote a circular letter to the family on July 16, 1930 (only one letter a month was allowed to a prisoner and a circular letter was a means of communicating with all of us):

> *Huzur Sahab* [a term used by the servants in addressing Mother, which Father used jokingly]: You are doing a little too much for your old bones. Use them sparingly if you wish to see *Swaraj* established in your lifetime.
>
> *Kamala:* Your letter is not as full as I expected it to be and there is no news of your health. Are you taking proper treatment and following the advice of Dr. Merse? The deputation which is preparing to meet us will, I am afraid, have to go back disappointed. Who are the people in charge of the Swaraj Bhawan? Please see that the house is not neglected.
>
> *Nan:* You seem to be too anxious to receive the "invitation." There would be some point in it if you could be lodged with us but that is impossible. You

would be increasing the trouble of those left behind by accepting an invitation too hurriedly. If it came in due time, as it is bound to come sooner or later for you all—I mean all except Bibima [our aunt] and the children—there is of course no helping it. But you need not meet it halfway.

Betti [my nickname]: How is it, Mademoiselle, that you have not sent us a line this week? Writing letters is your special gift. Why deprive your poor father of the fruit of it? I hope you are all right, otherwise someone would have said that you are not. Let me repeat to you the caution I have given to Nan about the invitation. Write in the sweet old strain you are accustomed to.

Indu [Indira]: What is your position in the Monkey Army? I suggest the wearing of a tail by every member, the length of which should be in proportion to the rank of the wearer. The badge with the print of Hanuman is all right but see that the *gada* which is usually in Hanuman's hand is not there. Remember the *gada* means violence and we are a nonviolent army. Have you got someone to teach you drilling and marching? It is essential. Above all you have to keep yourself fit. Practice running. Papu [her father] runs two miles every morning. You ought to be able to run at least one mile without stopping. Increase the distance gradually. I used to walk on the slope which separates the low lands of our garden from other parts and had them measured, but I have forgotten the measurements. You can have it measured again and find out how many lengths of it make a mile. Then begin running twice or thrice along the walk, as much as you can do without getting tired or out of breath. Go on increasing gradually, say half a length every two or three days. In this way you will soon be able to run a mile without getting tired or losing breath.

—MOTILAL NEHRU

The strain of living in a prison cell took its toll. Jawahar was able to give devoted nursing care to Father (they occupied adjoining cells), but Father's health deteriorated rapidly, and he was released in September. Mother, Nan, and I took him to the hills of Mussoorie for recuperation. Kamala was busy with Congress activities in Allahabad, and therefore she and Indira remained at Anand Bhawan. On Jawahar's release a few weeks later, he and Kamala joined us in Mussoorie. But when we returned to Allahabad, Jawahar was arrested once again and sentenced to two and a half years for a speech he had made.

There were protest meetings throughout the country. Mother, Nan, and I attended a meeting where Kamala read out the very speech for which Jawahar had received his sentence of an unduly long imprisonment. She was arrested.

Toward the end of January, 1931, Father was on his deathbed. Kamala, Jawahar, Gandhiji, Ranjit (Nan's husband), and all members of the Congress Working Committee were released from prison. Father sat up to receive visitors. Though in terrible pain, his power of self-control enabled him to speak to us with a clear mind.

Man doth not yield himself to the angels, nor even unto death utterly, save by the weakness of his feeble will.

—EDGAR ALLAN POE

Father died on February 6. Gandhiji consoled mother in her supreme sorrow. We all grieved at the loss of a wonderful father and grandfather. Anand Bhawan would no longer ring with his laughter. But to all of us he left a proud heritage: courage and the will never to surrender to weakness.

On April 21, 1931, Jawahar wrote a letter to comfort Indira (she was with him and her mother that day, on board ship on their voyage to Ceylon):

We sorrow for him and miss him at every step. And as the days go by the sorrow does not seem to grow less or his absence more tolerable. But, then, I think that he would not have us so. He would not like us to give in to grief, but to face it, as he faced his troubles, and conquer it. He would like us to go on with the work he left unfinished. How can we rest or give in to futile grief when work beckons and the cause of India's freedom demands our service? For that cause he died. For that cause we will live and strive and, if necessary, die. After all, we are his children and have something of his fire and strength and determination in us.[8]

6

History Lessons from a Father in Prison

INDIRA ATTENDED a convent school in Delhi for a while and then entered a day school in Allahabad. But she never had continuous schooling. Jawahar, in prison, supplemented her education by means of correspondence. It was on her tenth birthday that he began a series of letters with the intent of providing direction to her thinking and learning. (These letters were published in Allahabad under the title *Letters From a Father to His Daughter*.) And because he wanted to give her a taste for history, his next series dealt with happenings in the world—from early man to present-day civilizations: ". . . how the world has slowly but surely progressed, how the first simple animals gave place to more complicated and advanced animals, how last of all came the master animal—Man, and how by force of his intellect he triumphed over the others."[1]

Indira loved her father's letters. They stimulated her to

read the books in our library. She had grown into a shy, serious, thin, long-legged, and delicate-looking teenager. Often she turned to me as someone to lean upon, and I hope this will never change.

In 1930, Jawahar—again behind prison bars at Naini—wrote a memorable letter:

> For Indira Priyadarshini on Her Thirteenth Birthday
>
> On your birthday you have been in the habit of receiving presents and good wishes. Good wishes you will still have in full measure, but what present can I send you from Naini Prison? My presents cannot be very material or solid. They can only be of the air and of the mind and spirit, such as a good fairy might have bestowed on you—things that even the high walls of prison cannot stop.
>
> You know, sweetheart, how I dislike sermonizing and doling out good advice. . . . And so I have always thought that the best way to find out what is right and what is not right, what should be done and what should not be done, is not by giving a sermon, but by talking and discussing, and out of discussion sometimes a little bit of the truth comes out. . . .
>
> So, if I say anything that sounds like good advice do not take it as if it were a bad pill to swallow. Imagine that I have made a suggestion to you for you to think over, as if we really were having a talk. . . .
>
> The year you were born in—1917—was one of the memorable years of history when a great leader, with a heart full of love and sympathy for the poor and suffering, made his people write a noble and never-to-be-forgotten chapter of history. In the very month in which you were born, Lenin started the great Revolution which has changed the face of Russia and

Siberia. And today in India another great leader, also full of love for all who suffer and passionately eager to help them, has inspired our people to great endeavour and noble sacrifice, so that they may again be free and the starving and the poor and the oppressed may have their burdens removed from them. . . . In India today we are making history, and you and I are fortunate to see this happening before our eyes and to take some part ourselves in this great drama. . . .

I cannot say what part will fall to our lot; but, whatever it may be, let us remember that we can do nothing which may bring discredit to our cause or dishonour to our people. . . . It is no easy matter to decide what is right and what is not. One little test I shall ask you to apply whenever you are in doubt. It may help you. Never do anything in secret or anything that you would wish to hide. For the desire to hide anything means that you are afraid, and fear is a bad thing and unworthy of you. . . .

Good-bye, little one, and may you grow up into a brave soldier in India's service.[2]

Indira did "grow up into a brave soldier in India's service."

In a letter written on New Year's Day, 1931, Jawahar put down more reflections on history and added a poignant note on the loneliness of separations:

History is one connected whole and you cannot understand even the history of any one country if you do not know what has happened in other parts of the world. . . . Remember always that there is not so very much difference between various people as we seem to imagine.

. . . I thought of Mummie and you. Later in the

morning came the news that Mummie had been arrested . . . and I have no doubt that Mummie is
thoroughly happy and contented.

But you must be rather lonely. Once a fortnight
you may see Mummie and once a fortnight you may
see me, and you will carry our messages to each
other. But I shall sit down with pen and paper and I
shall think of you. And then you will silently come
near me and we shall talk of many things. And we
shall dream of the past, and find our way to make the
future greater than the past.[3]

Jawahar's release from prison due to Father's illness put
a temporary stop to his letter-writing. Soon after Father's
death, Gandhiji went to Delhi for conversations with Lord
Irwin. They concluded the famous Delhi Pact (also called
the Gandhi-Irwin Pact). Many of us felt bitterly disappointed with the agreement because it halted the *Satyagraha*
campaign. Thus the elation of our great struggle was ended
"not with a bang but a whimper."

At the next session of the Congress, held at Karachi,
Gandhiji presented an interpretation of the clauses of the
Pact, and Jawahar offered a resolution to ratify it. But in
his speech he also expressed his reservations about it.

After the Karachi Congress, Jawahar's health broke
down, and the doctors recommended a rest and a change
of scene. With Kamala and Indira, he sailed from Bombay
for Ceylon on a month's holiday. Eleven months later,
once again in prison, Jawahar resumed the correspondence course in history for Indira with a letter seeking to
recapture the "glorious holiday." His remembrance of
happy days with Indira and Kamala intensified his need
to communicate with his daughter.

Meanwhile the civil disobedience movement had started again, and even before Gandhiji returned from the second Round Table Conference in London, many of the leaders were arrested in breach of the Pact, and the Indian National Congress was declared illegal. Kamala, lying ill in Bombay, was inconsolable about not being able to join the ranks of the fighters. Nan and I worked like beavers for the cause; we were arrested and sentenced to fifteen months imprisonment. Mother marched in a procession and was seriously injured when the police knocked her down and hit her repeatedly on the head with a cane.

At home there was the problem of schooling for Indira and for Nan's three young daughters. Swaraj Bhawan (the Congress headquarters) had been seized by the government, and there was talk about a possible confiscation of Anand Bhawan. Gandhiji suggested a boarding school in Poona—called Pupils' Own School—run by a nationalist Parsi couple, Mr. and Mrs. Vakil, whom he knew. So the four children were sent to Poona.

The first days at school were almost unbearable for Indira. She was homesick. At night she could be heard sobbing in bed. But the feeling of sadness and longing for her parents was assuaged by Mrs. Vakil. Besides, she knew that her family would frown upon such a display of weakness. And the letters from her father reminded her of the gentleness and concern for others in her home environment. So she took a hand in looking after the younger children—helping them to dress and comb their hair, and guiding them in their lessons.

As a student she was conscientious, hard-working, and intelligent. She was especially good in English and history, and proficient in French, which she had learned in Switzerland. Being unusually well read, well informed on politics, and well equipped for leadership (as shown in her dealings with the Monkey Army), she contributed a great deal to the cultural programs of the school. She also participated in games and sports and acted in school plays. She became the most popular student with both teachers and students. Her knowledge of politics and her excellence in school debates resulted in a school mock parliament electing her the prime minister.

Indira and her three cousins called on Gandhiji, who was in Yeravda prison in Poona. In September, 1932, he had begun a "fast unto death" in protest against the British government's communal award granting a separate electorate to the depressed classes of India. This social injustice, which the British were trying to make into a permanent political fact, aroused the people and led to a tremendous upheaval. The Indian National Congress undertook to work for the removal of untouchability. Gandhiji's fast led to the Poona Pact. The British minister, influenced by the widespread violent commotion, agreed to the Pact, and Gandhiji's fast was broken.

On the visit of the four girls, Gandhiji, ever mindful of Jawahar's longing for his daughter, sent him a telegram: "Saw Indu [and] Swarup's children. Indu looked happy and in possession of more flesh. Doing very well."[4]

Early in 1933, Nan and I were released from prison. We went to Calcutta with mother to see Kamala, who was under treatment there. Then we went to Poona for a delightful week with Nan's children and Indira.

Jawahar's two-year prison term was drawing to a close —and so his teaching of world history by correspondence also drew to a close. On August 9, 1933, he sent Indira the final lesson, a charming letter with apt quotations from statesmen, philosophers, and poets:

> We have finished, my dear; the long story has ended. I need write no more, but the desire to end off with a kind of flourish induces me to write another letter—the Last Letter! . . .
>
> It is easy to admire the beauties of the universe and to live in a world of thought and imagination. But to try to escape in this way from the unhappiness of others, caring little what happens to them, is no sign of courage or fellow-feeling. Thought, in order to justify itself, must lead to action. "Action is the end of thought," says our friend Romain Rolland. "All thought which does not look towards action is an abortion and a treachery. If then we are the servants of thought we must be the servants of action." . . .
>
> We have finished, *carissima*, and this last letter ends. The last letter! Certainly not. I shall write you many more. But this series ends, and so
>
> *Tamām Shud!*[5]

On his homecoming, Jawahar had to face yet another family problem. I had asked Nan to tell him that I had chosen my future husband. My brother's reaction to this news was described in my book *With No Regrets*.

> When Jawahar spoke to me about Raja, he did so in a very characteristic way. With a twinkle in his eye he said, "Well, my dear, I hear you are contemplating marriage. Could you enlighten me somewhat about the young man?" I felt rather embar-

rassed, but I said I would. Jawahar started asking me what Raja did. I told him he was a barrister and had just started practicing. Then Jawahar asked who Raja's people were and I said I had not the faintest idea. . . . Jawahar, not quite upset, said, "This is preposterous."[6]

Jawahar hastened to Bombay to meet his prospective brother-in-law and came back with his consent. Raja Hutheesing and I were married at Anand Bhawan on October 20, 1933.

Jawahar knew that his release from prison would be short-lived. The period of freedom gave him a chance to attain two goals: to be with Kamala as much as possible and to provide for Indira's future education. "I was wholly against her joining the regular official or semi-official universities," he wrote, "for I disliked them. The whole atmosphere that envelops them is official, oppressive, and authoritarian."[7]

In January, 1934, he and Kamala went to Calcutta for a consultation with physicians concerning further treatment for Kamala. From Calcutta they went to visit Rabindranath Tagore and the university he had founded at Santiniketan. They decided that Indira should join this institution.

Three years of a formal course of study at the Pupils' Own School in Poona had been good for Indira. In 1934 she passed the matriculation examination and was entered at Santiniketan. This great international university concentrated on literature, music, art, and dancing. Students came from all over the world. They lived a simple and austere life, which included care of their rooms and other domestic chores. Indira developed an interest in art and dancing. She learned the Manipuri style of dancing and performed a solo in one of the famous dance plays of Tagore.

Indira's first year at Santinkiketan was nearing its end when suddenly she had to leave. Kamala's condition had become worse, and the doctors advised treatment at a sanatorium in Badenweiler, Germany. With Jawahar in prison, Indira took on the responsibility of accompanying her sick mother. Tagore wrote to Jawahar:

> It is with a heavy heart that we bade farewell to Indira, for she was such an asset in our place. I watched her very closely and have felt admiration for the way you brought her up. Her teachers all in one voice praise her and I know she is extremely popular with the students. I only hope things will turn for the better and she will soon return here.[8]

Indira recognizes what she owes to Santiniketan, for Tagore gave her a love of art and poetry.

7

"All Our Bright Dreams"

FOR FIVE MONTHS and thirteen days—from late August, 1933, to February 12, 1934—Kamala and Jawahar had been together. During these blissful months, spent in Calcutta, at Santiniketan with Tagore, and in Allahabad, they had felt very near and dear to each other. Kamala was in high spirts and seemed to be in good health.

Then prison again claimed Jawahar. He was taken to the Alipore jail in Calcutta, and on May 7 was transferred to Dehra Dun. It was here that he began writing his autobiography—partly as a diversion from the depression of imprisonment and partly to answer his own questions about what had actually happened in India.

By July, Kamala was very ill. Her condition became critical, and Jawahar was taken to Allahabad under police escort. Indira came from Santiniketan. Jawahar was shocked to see Kamala very weak and wasted away. Dedicated to a common ideal, they had grown to know and rely upon each other. Kamala was a source of great comfort to Jawahar and never let him know how ill she had become and how much she needed him. She was always optimistic, and whenever she was near Jawahar, she soothed him and infused new courage into him at moments of anxiety and disillusionment.

Jawahar was allowed to remain with his wife for eleven days. His presence and tender care cheered Kamala so much that she showed improvement. But as soon as the British government in India, which had asked for daily bulletins from the physicians, learned of her having passed the critical stage, the police were sent to take Jawahar to the Naini prison, which was only eight miles from Anand Bhawan. The British considered him to be dangerous and therefore wanted to keep him in safe custody. He left with a heavy heart. His wife's brave smile as she bade him good-bye haunted him.

After his departure Kamala's condition worsened. By September her life was again in danger. The government offered to release Jawahar if he would give them an assurance to refrain from political activity. He refused, even though he knew that he could hardly leave his wife long enough to engage in politics. However, in October the police delivered him to Allahabad once more. He found Kamala a shadow of herself, with a high temperature. But in the brief bedside visit that he was permitted, she mustered enough strength to whisper, "What is this about your giving an assurance to Government? Do not give it!"[1]

The doctors, believing that pure air and a bracing climate might do Kamala good, put her in a sanatorium in

Bhowali, a small station in wooded mountains that gave a view of the snowy peaks of the Himalayas. In the cold invigorating air, she grew better. The government was considerate enough to transfer Jawahar to the Almora District jail, which was not far from Bhowali. In three and a half months he was allowed to visit his wife five times.

Dr. Madan Atal, a cousin of ours, was in constant attendance on Kamala. In May, 1935, he decided that the best course of treatment could be obtained in the Badenweiler Sanatorium in Germany's Black Forest. Thus it came about that Indira left Santiniketan to take her mother to Badenweiler and to stay with her. The faithful Dr. Atal accompanied them.

There they were joined from time to time by a young Parsi, Feroze Gandhi (he was not related to Mahatma Gandhi), who would come over from London whenever he could leave his classes at the London School of Economics. He was an ardent admirer of Kamala. She had been responsible for enlisting him in the civil disobedience movement as a Congress Volunteer.

Kamala and I had become acquainted with him when we were in a group of women picketing a college. The boys of the college—Feroze was one of them—were sitting on top of a campus wall watching us. We shouted slogans at them and asked them to give up attendance at a college that was a government institution and to join the national movement.

It was an extremely hot day, but we picketed for hours under the blazing sun, longing for a drink of water. It was customary for onlookers of such demonstrations to serve water, but those boys made no effort to do so. They were merely amused and looked on us as a big joke. Suddenly

Kamala fainted. The students jumped down from the wall and ran over to us. They carried her to the shade of a tree, went for water, and put a wet cloth on her brow. Someone brought a *punkha* (fan) to cool her face. When Kamala recovered, we took her home.

This event changed the mood and outlook of the students. The next day many of them, including Feroze, left the college and registered at the Congress office as Volunteers. Feroze was so impressed by Kamala's devotion to *Satyagraha* and her physical bravery that he attached himself to her. As president of a district committee, she often had to travel from village to village, and he would carry her picnic basket of sandwiches and tea. He became her constant companion as she went about her work.

And so, when he heard of Kamala's being taken for treatment to Europe, he persuaded his rich aunt to send him to England to study. To Indira, he became a tower of strength in her solicitude for her mother.

Jahawar, still in the mountain jail of Almora, was tormented by anxiety about both Kamala and Indira. The days dragged on until one day there came a telegram (it was a delayed telegram, for the government, as usual, had intercepted delivery) informing him that Kamala was failing rapidly. On September 4, 1935, he was informed that his remaining sentence of six months was suspended. The next day he reached Allahabad, and from there flew to Europe. It was a five-day journey, with landings in various cities and transport by train. He reached Badenweiler on September 9.

As he sat by her bedside from day to day, and on his walks through the Black Forest he thought of the brave and energetic part Kamala had played in *Satyagraha*. Ten years later he was to record the thoughts he had in those dark days:

> A hundred pictures of Kamala succeeded each other in my mind, a hundred aspects of her rich and deep personality. We had been married for nearly twenty years, and yet how many times she had surprised me by something new in her mental or spiritual make-up. I had known her in so many ways, and, in later years, I had tried my utmost to understand her. That understanding had not been denied to me, but I often wondered if I really knew her or understood her. There was something elusive about her, something faylike, real but unsubstantial, difficult to grasp. . . .
>
> My past life unrolled itself before me and there was always Kamala, standing by. She became a symbol of Indian women, or of woman herself. . . . How fortunate we were, I told her and she agreed, for though we had sometimes quarreled and grown angry with each other, we had kept that vital spark alight, and for each one of us life was always unfolding new adventure and giving fresh insight into the other.[2]

Kamala surprised us by regaining some of her old vitality. After Christmas she said that she was weary of Badenweiler and wanted a change of environment. Dr. Atal agreed to her wish, and at the end of January, 1936, she was taken to a sanatorium near Lausanne, Switzerland.

Again Kamala's condition improved. Indira went back to the school she had once attended at Bex (it was not far from Lausanne). And Jawahar, who had again been elected president of the Indian National Congress, planned to fly to India for the April session. Four days before his planned departure, Kamala grew worse. With Jawahar, Indira, and Feroze at her bedside, Kamala died on February 28, 1936, and she was cremated in Lausanne.

To help Indira recover from grief over the loss of her mother, Jawahar took her to the lakeside resort of Montreux for a few days of gentle and tender conversation. She then returned to the school at Bex, and he flew back to India.

On the flight, as he wrote eight years later from the Ahmadnagar Fort prison, "a terrible loneliness gripped me and I felt empty and purposeless. I was going back alone to my home, which was no longer home for me, and there by my side was a basket and that basket contained an urn. That was all that remained of Kamala, and all our bright dreams were also dead and turned to ashes. She is no more, Kamala is no more, my mind kept on repeating."[3]

When he reached Baghdad, he sent a cable to the publishers of his autobiography in London. He submitted a dedication: "To Kamala who is no more."

At Karachi he was met by crowds. "And then Allahabad, where we carried the precious urn to the swift-flowing Ganga and poured the ashes into the bosom of that noble river."[4]

It hurt me to see him so aged and grief-stricken. His sad eyes were full of the agony in his heart.

8

"*Life Grows Harder*"

AFTER A SHORT TERM at Bex, Indira went to England to enter the Badminton School at Bristol to prepare herself for the London matriculation examination, for Jawahar wanted her to go up to Oxford University. There was no point in her returning to India and getting involved in politics, which, after the withdrawal of the civil disobedience movement, was at a low ebb. She saw a great deal of Feroze, who was at the London School of Economics. After Bristol, she attended Somerville College, Oxford. But politics was in her blood and she could not stay away from it. On trips to London she worked for the India League under Krishna Menon—sometimes to raise funds for India's Spanish Aid Committee or the China Aid Committee (her father had organized and was president of both). Or she would come down to London just to see the Spanish actress La Pasionaria.

In 1937–38, Europe was in turmoil. Hitler had begun his aggressions on neighboring countries. Spain was plunged in a civil war. In America and Europe a new spirit of liberal thought was drawing the young to join the International Brigade to rescue the Spanish Republic. For Indian students, being in Europe at this time was exciting. They were already *au courant* with their own freedom movement, and in the free atmosphere of England they could see what freedom means to a people who can openly proclaim that they will not fight for "king and country," as the Oxford Students Union did. Such open manifestations strengthened Indira's faith in the ultimate victory of India's struggle.

Though many people knew that Jawahar's daughter was in England and would have liked to have gotten to know her, she generally kept to herself. However, she could always turn for companionship to the ever loyal Feroze.

Another close friend was an Indian girl, Shanta Gandhi, who had been a student with her at the Pupils' Own School in Poona. In London they met often and at times shared rooms. Apart from their ardent nationalism, they had much in common. Shanta, like Indira, knew Indian dancing and often performed for the shows given in support of Spanish aid. Indira would sell tickets or help in other ways. One day Indira introduced her to Feroze, and Shanta claims that she guessed they were in love. Perhaps Indira's marriage to Feroze in 1942 led Shanta to imagine that she had recognized their being in love in those student days, but Indira, like a true Nehru, does not show her feelings.

Because of her father's long-standing friendships with

eminent Europeans, Indira had opportunities to meet wonderful people. While a student at Oxford she renewed her acquaintance with Ernst Toller and his wife Christine, whom she had met in Switzerland in 1927. Now they were refugees from Hitler. In Ernst Toller's eyes, Indira saw anguish. He had been a revolutionary leader in Germany ever since the post-World War I period, and Indira found in his talk deep humanism and love of freedom. His great play *Man and the Masses* reflected the struggle of man's conscience against violence. The Tollers' affection for Indira was expressed in a letter Christine wrote to Jawahar: "Not only that she is so beautiful but so pure which makes one feel happy. She seemed to me like a little flower which the wind blows away so easily, but I think she is not afraid of the wind."[1] The Tollers left England to settle in the United States; in 1939, Ernst Toller committed suicide. To Indira he symbolized the Hitler victims.

Jawahar was again deeply involved in Congress activities. In 1937 he was re-elected President. The British government had produced a new constitution for India—after three Round Table Conferences that sought to give a semblance of power to the legislatures in the provinces while giving nothing at the center. The constitution was unacceptable to the Congress, which decided to contest the elections and form ministries in the provinces if they won the majorities. Jawahar, though he did not approve of the policy, threw himself into the campaign and traveled the length and breadth of the country in the interest of the Congress candidates. It was a "voyage of discovery," for though he loved his country, "he knew little of its people and their culture which had survived through centuries and held them together."

His thoughts often dwelt on his daughter, and in speeches he made touching references to her. Once, speaking to Pathan tribesmen, he said:

> I have a daughter, twenty years of age, who is far away in England. She is my only child and she is dear to me. I have tried to teach her courage and self-reliance and to keep no company with fear whatever might happen. If she were with me here now, I would ask her unhesitatingly to go unaccompanied into the tribal territories, and to visit the people there, and make friends with them. I would do so having faith in her and faith in those people.[2]

Jawahar had now finished two successive terms as President of the Congress. At the close of the 1937 term, he retired from the presidency.

Early in 1938, I took my two small sons to Allahabad for our annual family gathering. Nan and her husband and children were already there, and Jawahar had returned from his journeys through India. We were all happy to be together, especially to be with Mother (she had had two strokes) and with our beloved aunt Bibi Amma, Mother's elder sister, who had given Mother the devotion of a lifetime. She had been widowed while still in her teens, and had lived with us as long as any of us could remember. We missed Indira, who was still in England.

Mother was gay and seemed quite well. But one evening as we sat around talking, she suddenly collapsed. Her doctor was called; he told us that she had had a massive stroke. All through the night, Jawahar, Nan, Bibi Amma, and I watched over her. She died in the morning.

As I put my arms around Bibi Amma, she said, "I lived

only for your mother and now my task is done." She died within twenty-four hours of Mother's death.

Jahawar was tired and lonely and desired to be with Indira. He sailed for Spain on June 2 and from there went to London to take Indira with him to Europe. Everywhere in their wide travels they found evidence of the fear inspired by Hitler. They observed the hopeless plight of Jews and all those who were politically opposed to Nazi Germany; Hitler's annexation of the Czech Sudetenland with its three million Germans; and the Munich Conference of September 29–30, 1938, when Britain and France broke their promises to Czechoslovakia and shamefully handed this free country over to Hitler. War clouds were gathering over Europe and the world. Jawahar returned to Allahabad in November, bringing Indira with him.

On the last leg of their journey, while crossing the Arabian Sea, Jawahar wrote one of those history-lesson letters to Indira. It was dated November 14, 1938. He called it a "Postscript" to the "Last Letter" written in 1933.

I am supposed to tell you in this Postscript the story of these five years, for these Letters are going to appear in a new garb, and my publisher demands that they should be brought up to date. . . .

The boundaries of democracy have to be widened now so as to include economic equality also. This is the great revolution through which we are all passing . . . to give democracy its full meaning, and to bring ourselves in line with the advance of science and technology.

This equality does not fit in with imperialism or with capitalism, which are based on inequality and the exploitation of nation or class. . . . The present world conflict is not between communism and social-ism on the one hand and fascism on the other. It is between democracy and fascism, and all the real forces of democracy line up and become anti-fasc-ists.[3]

By the end of November, Indira, possibly owing to ex-haustion from the extensive travels abroad, was not well. A winter in the hills, said Jawahar, would restore her strength, and he asked me to take my three- and four-year-old sons and go with her to the Almora resort in the Himalayas, where he had engaged a cottage. In the vast silence of the mountains, Indira and I passed the time reading, discussing the philosophies of the wonderful peo-ple we had met, and watching the children play in the snow. Occasionally we had visitors—European artists and the Indian scientist Boshi Sen and his American wife. It was an altogether delightful winter.

The whole family attended the Congress session held at Tripura in March, 1939. It was an exciting session. Subhas Chandra Bose, up for re-election as President, was op-posed by Gandhiji, who supported the nominee of the Congress Working Committee. Jawahar, too, opposed Bose, who advocated collaboration with the totalitarian states, believing that they would help India gain inde-pendence. Though the Working Committee was sullen and clashes occurred, Bose was re-elected. One month later he was forced to resign, through Gandhiji's influ-ence.

Indira returned to Oxford in April, 1939. She enjoyed her courses and the associations of college life. Among writers she met was Edward J. Thompson (he had au-

thored several books on India). In December he wrote to
Jawahar from England:

> I have seen Indu. She looks well and she is *well*.
> She is thin of course, and there seems no doubt that
> just now she is what used to be called "delicate" and
> will have to go carefully. But she is wiry underneath
> and when she is past these difficult days that end
> adolescence, she will pull into real strength.[4]

But in 1940 she fell ill with pleurisy and was taken to a
London hospital. The doctors, familiar with her mother's
medical history, feared that the inflammatory processes
might lead to tuberculosis and therefore suggested that
after her discharge from the hospital it would be advisa-
ble for her to seek the dry and sunny climate of Switzerland.

I was terribly upset and wanted to rush off to be with
her, but Raja was against this as the war made sea travel
hazardous. Then a reassuring letter came from Jawahar:

> I have just had a cable from Indu. It was a birth-
> day cable but she added good news about herself.
> For the last 19 days she has had no temperature and
> the inflammation has subsided. She has put on 5 lbs.
> in weight. So, she has progressed satisfactorily but
> she will remain in hospital for another two weeks.
> After that she will go to Switzerland—either Leysin
> or somewhere near Davos. Probably Agatha will ac-
> company her there but will not remain with her. The
> doctors intend keeping her there four or five months.
> After that one does not know where the world will
> be or any of us.

But the war enforced an extension of the "four or five
months" in Switzerland. It became inadvisable to return

to Oxford, for Germany's bombing of the cities of England had risen to a crescendo. In early 1941, Indira decided to return home, for she knew that the struggle for freedom in India was being reactivated.

The Congress had started individual *Satyagraha* in protest against the declaration of war that the Viceroy issued on behalf of India without consulting our people and granting us our right to freedom and democracy. The Congress Working Committee said that India in bondage could not fight a war in support of Great Britain. Gandhiji had chosen Jawahar as the second *Satyagrahi* (after Vinobha Bhave), and he was to offer the *Satyagraha* on November 7, 1940, after informing the government that he would address a public meeting advising the people not to cooperate with the war effort. But the government, as usual, dealt with the problem in advance by arresting Jawahar on October 31, as he was returning from a meeting with Gandhiji, and sentenced him to four years imprisonment for three speeches he had made a month before. And so he was back in prison at Dehra Dun.

When I learned of Indira's decision to come home, I felt nervous about her traveling by sea, since many ships were being sunk by German submarines. So I wrote to Jawahar hoping that he would dissuade her. He replied from prison chiding me for my fears:

> I am glad she has decided to return. There are all manner of risks and dangers of course, but it is better to face them than to feel isolated and miserable. If she wants to return then she must do so or take the consequences. Life grows harder for all of us and the soft days of the past already belong to an age that is gone. When will they return? No one knows. Or will they return? We must adapt ourselves to life as it is

and not hunger for what is not. Physical risk and suffering are often all petty compared to the troubles and tempests of the mind. And whether life is soft or hard, one can always get something out of it—but to enjoy life ultimately one must decide not to count the costs.

Indira's homeward journey—via Antibes, Barcelona, Lisbon, and England, where Feroze helped her secure passage on a troop ship that sailed around the Cape of Good Hope—exposed her to all the perils of war.

En route the ship docked at Durban for a week. Aware of the apartheid policy of the South African government, Indira remained on board ship. But the large Indian community in Durban, hearing that Jawahar's daughter was on the ship, insisted on arranging a public reception for her. She refused. They took her round the city sightseeing, and so she saw how the Negroes lived under the apartheid policy. Moved by what she had seen, she accepted the invitation to a reception and delivered a speech, in which she said that if the Indians wanted to live in South Africa they must identify themselves with the people to whom the country belonged—namely, the Negroes. She condemned the Indian community's attitude of servility to the white rulers and its acceptance of the apartheid policy, which she compared to the Nazi racial persecution. The Indian community, frightened of the consequences of the speech, avoided Indira for the rest of the ship's stay in Durban.

In June, Indira arrived in Bombay, where Raja and I had our home. She looked frail and ill. The first thing she did was to visit her father in prison, and then she went to Anand Bhawan, which must have seemed very dismal without her father, mother, grandmother, and great-aunt Bibi Amma. Jawahar, worried about her health, saw to it that she had a medical check-up. At the suggestion of her doctors he rented a cottage for her in Mussoorie, a mountain resort. He asked me to join her with my two sons, then aged seven and six. We had an enjoyable and restful summer, and Indira's health improved. I left for Bombay in October, but Indira remained so that she could visit her father in the Dehra Dun prison, which was not far from Mussoorie.

9

A Marriage
That Raised a Storm

ON ONE OF HER VISITS to her father in prison, Indira told him that she wanted to marry Feroze Gandhi. Feroze's family lived in Allahabad, so he was constantly in and out of Anand Bhawan.

The surname Gandhi owes its origin, as do many surnames in India, to the trade or profession followed by the family. At the time of its adoption, the name Gandhi referred to one who was a grocer or a provisions merchant and not to caste or community. Mahatma Gandhi was a Hindu and no relation to Feroze, who was a Parsi.

The Parsis are Zoroastrians by religion and follow the prophet Zoroaster, who, they believe, brought sacred fire down from heaven. They therefore worship fire, and their temples are called Fire Temples. They originally came to India from Persia (about twelve hundred years ago according to some historians), seeking refuge from religious, persecution of the Muslim conquerors of their country. It is said that they came by sea in various batches, but there is no authentic history about their migration to India or the number of men and women who came. Some say that there was only one batch of five hundred men and no women, while others contend that there were at least five thousand men and twenty women. In any case, it is accepted that they landed at a port called Sanjana, near the large and prosperous town of Surat on the west coast of India. Sanjana at the time was ruled by a Hindu ruler, Rana of Sanjana, and the Parsis approached him for permission to settle there and requested that they be allowed to marry among the local population. The Rana agreed to give them his protection provided they accepted his conditions. They were asked to consider the cow as sacred, to include some of the Hindu religious customs in their marriage rites. The Parsis readily agreed to these conditions, and to this day they have kept their word.

There are only about 150,000 Parsis in India today, and most of them live in Bombay and the nearby district of Bulsar. They are hard-working and enterprising people and have a leading place in industry and in such professions as law and medicine. They have been called the Jews of India. Being a small community, they hold fast to old customs and religious observances. They can be found today in all important towns of India as provision and wine merchants.

When Jawahar learned from Indira that she wished to marry Feroze, he was somewhat upset. It was not because Feroze belonged to a different faith or religion. Our family had never considered caste, religion, or nationality as a barrier. Both my sister and I had married non-

Kashmiris; two of our cousins have married Muslims; and one cousin has married a Hungarian. Jawahar's opposition to the marriage was based on other reasons. First of all, he felt that Feroze's background and upbringing were too different from ours. We had been brought up according to Western ways and standards and had often argued about arranged marriages when some cousin or friend was getting married. Mother came from an Orthodox Hindu family, but Father had explained that it did not matter whom one married so long as the background of the families was the same. In India marriages continue to be arranged even today. Parents get the young people together from families they know but leave the final decision to the young couple. If the parental choice is not acceptable, the parents bring around other prospects.

Secondly, Jawahar felt that Indira's having been abroad a long time had precluded her meeting other young men in India. In London, of course, she had seen a great deal of one Indian—Feroze. At Oxford she was too reserved to make new friends, and she preferred to associate with old friends. When she returned to India in November, 1938 (she left again for Oxford in April, 1939), we were all involved in the national movement, and there was no time for social life.

Jawahar suggested to Indira that she should postpone a final decision and take advantage of the present opportunity to meet other young men. But Indira had made up her mind, and so he advised her to consult Nan and me.

Nan, whom Indira consulted first, presented arguments against the marriage. She stressed tradition, culture, and so on.

Then Indira came to Bombay to stay for a few days and talk things over with us. Raja told her that if she was really fond of Feroze and loved him, she should go ahead and marry him. My advise was the same as my brother's. I cautioned her not to make a lifetime's decision too quickly. As a reply she gave my own marriage as an example.

"You and Rajabhai," she said, "knew each other only ten days, at the end of which you decided to get married. Rajabhai might have known something about you, but you knew nothing about him. Chitti [she calls me Chitti, which is Tamil, though *Puphi* is the word for aunt in Hindi], I have known Feroze for a number of years and know him well. I have met many other Indian young men abroad, and I do not see why I should go out of my way to meet some more now. Besides, I wish to marry Feroze." It was a logical answer.

Jawahar was released from prison on December 4, 1941. On December 7, Japan attacked Pearl Harbor. The next day the United States and Britain declared war on Japan. With the opening of the new front in Asia, the British were hard pressed. On December 11 the United States declared war on Germany and Italy. The entrance of the United States on the side of the Allies raised the British confidence in ultimate victory. For India this meant that Britain would be in a less compromising mood, for had not Mr. Churchill said that he had not become the Prime Minister to liquidate the British Empire? President Roosevelt's Four Freedoms and the Atlantic Charter (it had been issued on August 14, 1941) were ignored as far as India was concerned. The war in Asia was becoming a reality to us, as the Japanese advance into Burma inflicted heavy defeats on the Dutch, the French, and the British forces.

With Jawahar out of prison, Indira and Feroze were

anxious to get married. Considering the situation in the country as well as their own inclination, they wanted a quiet wedding. But before anything could be arranged, news of their engagement leaked out, and people who had nothing to do with us raised a hue and cry. Anonymous angry letters from Hindu and Parsi orthodoxy poured in; they protested against this intercommunity marriage and threatened all sorts of dire consequences. Jawahar issued a public statement on his views:

> A marriage is a personal and domestic matter, affecting chiefly the two parties concerned and partly their families. . . . I have long held the view that though parents should advise in the matter, the choice and the ultimate decision must be with the two parties concerned. That decision, if arrived at after mature deliberation, must be given effect to, and it is no business of the parents or others to come in the way. When Indira and Feroze wanted to marry each another, I accepted willingly their decision and told them that it had my blessing.

Jawahar had consulted Gandhiji, as he had done when I married. After Father's death Gandhiji had taken his place in our family, and we looked to him for guidance. Because this was widely known, Gandhiji also received abusive and threatening letters, so Gandhiji advised Indira that the marriage should be a fairly big affair, even though he preferred a simple ceremony, because "otherwise people would think that your father was unwilling to stand by you and that would be unfair to your father and to you." So Indira agreed to a somewhat elaborate wedding.

Nan had married a non-Kashmiri, but her husband was a Brahmin and so the marriage was performed according to Hindu religious rites. My own case was different. Raja is a Jain, and though Jains are a part of the Hindu fold, I, a Brahmin, could not marry him under the Hindu rites but had to have a civil registration marriage for it to be legally valid. Under the then existing Hindu law, a Brahmin male, being of the highest caste, could marry a woman of any caste, because his wife would be elevated to the high caste. But a Brahmin woman could not marry a man from a lower caste. My mother was not too happy about my civil marriage. She had hoped that at a later date we would have a proper Hindu ceremony.

Indira's wedding was fixed for March, 1942. It could not be as grand or spectacular as her father's, nor as elaborate as my sister's. My wedding was a very simple and unostentatious one, for my mother was very ill at the time. The civil registration was arranged in our sitting room, which was beautifully decorated with flowers. The actual ceremony took no more than ten minutes. To this day my husband says he does not feel married. But Indira's wedding was to be by Vedic rites and would take more than an hour and a half. A big *shamiana* (cloth canopy) was put up. Many guests came from all over the country.

The wedding day was a bright and beautiful March morning. Indira wore a pale pink sari embroidered with tiny silver flowers. The sari had been woven from yarn spun by her father during one of his prison terms. Instead of jewelry she wore ornaments made of flowers, which is the Kashmiri custom. She looked calm as usual, but the glow of her face disclosed an inner excitement. Always lovely to look at, she looked lovelier than ever—frail and ethereal.

It was a simple and beautiful Vedic ceremony. At the appointed time, Jawahar escorted Indira to the *shamiana*, where Feroze, with his family, awaited her. He was dressed in a *khadi sherwani* (knee-length coat) and *churidar* (tight-fitting pajamas), as is the North Indian custom. The bride and groom sat side by side in front of the sacred fire. Next to the bride sat her father, and beside him there was a vacant seat, with a brocade cushion on it, as a symbol of the bride's mother, who was no more. To the bride and groom, the vacant seat was a reminder that there is no happiness without a touch of sorrow. Jawahar placed the hand of his daughter in the hand of the groom. With their hands clasped, they took the traditional Seven Steps round the fire while repeating the marriage vows after the priest.

Indira and Feroze had a short honeymoon in Kashmir. One day Indira, thinking of her lonely father in Anand Bhawan in the sweltering heat of the plains, sent him a telegram, "Wish we could send you some cool breezes from here." Jawahar sent a reply, "Thanks, but you have no mangoes." He knew how much Indira loved mangoes, which grew in abundance in Allahabad.

Indira and Feroze returned to settle in Allahabad. For a brief time they led a carefree and happy life in their lovely home, but soon both of them were deeply absorbed in politics and involved in arrests—the August imprisonment of Jawahar and Nan, and their own in September.

10

A British Mission to India

FACED WITH THE JAPANESE THREAT to India, Great Britain wanted India to participate in the war. In 1942 the British war cabinet sent Sir Stafford Cripps, a Labour member of the British Parliament, on a mission to India to win over the Congress for the Allied cause. Sir Stafford had been in India in 1939, and Jawahar and the Congress had liked and respected him for his integrity and ability. He had been a dinner guest in our home, and we had admired him for his simplicity and straightforward discussions.

The Cripps mission offered India the following proposals, to be effective *after* the cessation of hostilities: dominion status and a constituent assembly to frame a constitution, and the right of individual provinces of India to opt out of the future dominion. For the immediate present, there was to be an enlargement of the Viceroy's Executive Council, with the addition of a few Indian representatives of various parties. Practically, these Indian members were not to have any real authority. It was a ludicrous offer, with its implications of a future partition of India and no voice in the defense of our country. With the Japanese knocking at our doors, the peril of invasion was great. The war can "only be fought on a popular basis," said the Congress.

The proposals were rejected. They had aroused widespread anger and resentment. At the same time, the defeat and humiliation of the British at the hands of the Japanese afforded us some consolation.

The Congress could not sit idly by and acquiesce in the Japanese occupation of India, which seemed imminent. Gandhiji, with his intimate knowledge of the pulse of the people, realized that the Congress must now mobilize the people. He issued a call for *Satyagraha*. In an article published in his paper *Harijan*, he addressed the British: "You have sat too long here for any good you have been doing. Depart and let us have done with you. In the name of God, go!" The Congress took up the call to action. At first Jawahar was reluctant to embarrass the British at this juncture, but he sensed the mood of the people and accepted Gandhiji's lead.

On August 7, 1942, the All India Congress Committee met in Bombay. Jawahar, Indira, and Feroze came to Bombay a few days before the meeting and stayed with us as usual. Our apartment had only three bedrooms, so Raja and I gave our room to Indira and Feroze and arranged to sleep in the nearby home of friends who had a spare bedroom. The children occupied the third bedroom.

All day we were at the meetings, though I rushed home from time to time to order food and to see that everything was comfortable for my brother, niece, and nephew-in-law. Between sessions, innumerable visitors came for discussions with my brother; the telephone and doorbell kept ringing all day. Often visitors would stay on for a meal, and menus had to be expandable. It was difficult for me and my cook, but I had been used to such a household since the beginning of the national movement. The excitement helped us to take things in stride.

During this momentous Congress meeting we expected the police to swoop down and arrest all the leaders before the Quit India Resolution could be passed. For the first few nights I therefore slept on a divan in our sitting room in case the police should turn up at an odd hour, as was their practice, to arrest my brother. But when nothing happened for several days, I decided on the night of August 8 to sleep comfortably in our friends' apartment. After the strenuous activities we were rather worn out. The resolution had been passed by the Congress that day at about 6 P.M., and we felt relaxed. As my brother was getting into his car on the way home, a stranger passed him a note informing him that all the leaders were to be arrested that night. We did not believe it, nor did we care if it did happen. Gandhiji had been given the same information, but he too refused to believe it. He was convinced that the Viceroy, considering the threat of invasion to the country, would not invite chaos.

That evening our home was crowded with visitors who came to discuss the future course of action. Among them were two journalists—one British and the other an American, Philip Talbot—who were friends of ours. (Philip is today ambassador of his country.) Most of the visitors stayed on to dinner, and we dispersed after midnight and went to bed. At about 5 A.M. our host knocked on our door to tell us that the police were in our flat. Raja and I hurried over. In spite of the blackout, our flat was all lit up.

I thought that only Jawahar was being arrested. Raja was collecting books for him to read in jail, but Indira, who had talked with the police, informed Raja that he too was under arrest. And so my brother and my husband were taken away. Indira, Feroze, and I followed them in a friend's car to find out where they were being taken. From a distance we could see cars going into the Victoria Terminus. The roads and entrances to the station were surrounded by the police. All the leaders, including Gandhiji, had been arrested.

Indira left by train for Allahabad. The day after her arrival, the police came to Anand Bhawan in the early dawn to arrest Nan. Indira was now left alone in Anand Bhawan with three young cousins, Nan's daughters. Feroze had quietly left for Lucknow to do underground work for the movement. She had no news of him. A warrant had been issued for his arrest, but his whereabouts were unknown.

One day Indira deliberately courted arrest. The students of a college had invited her to attend the hoisting of the Congress flag. She knew that this was forbidden and that participants might be arrested. On her arrival, she saw the police beating the students with *lathis*. One of the boys fell bleeding to the ground, still holding on to the flag. Indira rushed to him, took the flag, and held it aloft. The students rallied around her, and then the police charged with their *lathis*. She was struck on her back, then on her hands, and she fell still clutching the flag. She would not let it go, for Nehrus will never surrender. Had not her father endured the batons of mounted police as he fell under the hoofs of their horses? Had not her grandmother, old and delicate, endured blows until she lay bleeding on the ground? Indira did not yield the precious flag.

That night Feroze came secretly to see her. He found her in good spirits because the flag had actually been hoisted in spite of the police. A few days later Indira called a meeting of Congress workers to give them news she had received about her father and other leaders. Rumors were spreading that the leaders had been spirited out of the country to the penal settlement on Andaman Island or to East Africa. Such rumors could undermine the people's resolve to carry on the civil disobedience movement nonviolently and lead to riots and killing. The British government of India was not averse to such a turn, for it would justify repressive measures and the detention of prisoners under concentration-camp conditions without first being brought before a court of law.

Public meetings were banned by the British, and Indira decided to defy the ban. A meeting could only be announced by word of mouth, since notices could not be published. But the grapevine is effective, and quite a crowd gathered to hear her. As Indira started her speech, a large contingent of the British army, their guns drawn, covered the audience. Indira continued to speak. A British officer lunged at her and ordered her to stop or else he would shoot. At that moment someone rushed forward and thrust himself between the officer and Indira. It was Feroze. The crowd also surged forward to protect her, and a scuffle ensued. Indira, Feroze, and many others were arrested.

In those days, setting out for prison produced elation. At a much later time, Indira was to recall how she felt: "I had made up my mind that I had to go to prison. Without that, you know, something would have been incomplete. So that I was glad to be arrested."[1]

Indira arrived at Naini prison to be greeted by her aunt Nan, who had already spent several weeks there. A few days later Lekha, Nan's eldest daughter, joined them. Nan kept a diary. It shows how Nehrus could create their own entertainment even in a sordid prison:

Sept. 13: Indu is going to help Lekha with her French.

Sept. 23: Indu was allowed to sleep outside last night—but she had a bad night in spite of it.

Sept. 26: We are told that Indu has been recommended for release on grounds of health. Her temperature persists.

Oct. 22: The Civil Surgeon came to see Indira today. He had been asked to see her and report on her health to Government.

Nov. 20: Yesterday was Indira's 25th birthday. She had her fortnightly interview with Feroze and came back from the office looking very happy.

Nov. 27: Indu and Lekha are both gifted with imagination and the evenings are seldom dull. The jail cat, named Mehitabel by Indu, has had four kittens, and Indu and Lekha are quited excited. After lockup Indu and Lekha read plays, each taking a part. I am the audience. It is very amusing.[2]

Indira's health continued to be very poor. She was released on May 13, 1943, along with Nan. An order was served on them to abide by restrictions on their movements and to refrain from taking part in processions or meetings. Both refused to give such assurance, and a week later Nan was rearrested. Indira was left alone because she had influenza. Jawahar, isolated in Ahmadnagar Fort, was worried about her being in the terrific heat of Allahabad and urged her to find relief in a resort in the hills. In a letter to me he wrote, "I suppose one of these days she will be taken to Naini [prison] to enjoy the heat and the other facilities which Naini so abundantly provides." Indira went to Panchgini, a hill station near Bombay, where she recovered from her illness. In August, when Feroze was released from prison, she left the resort to go home to Allahabad. At last she and her husband could be together.

India was undergoing a period of disaster, for a famine in Bengal had led to the death of millions of people by starvation. The streets of Calcutta were strewn with victims, living and dead. Nan, who had again been released, went to Calcutta to help in relief work, but tragedy struck and she rushed home. Ranjitbhai, her husband, had pneumonia, which had been brought on by appalling prison conditions. He died in Lucknow on January 14, 1944.

11

Indira's Firstborn

EARLY IN JANUARY, Indira was expecting her first child. She came to Bombay in March to live with us for the duration of her pregnancy and confinement. Feroze was back in prison, so I insisted that she should not stay alone in Anand Bhawan. Indira wanted to take advantage of the medical facilities in Bombay, and she wanted to be near me. Dr. Shirodkar, a well-known gynecologist, gave her a complete physical examination. Then we all went to Matheran, a hill station about twenty-seven miles from Bombay.

One afternoon we heard a distant but loud rumble. Indira thought it must be an army of monkeys jumping on the galvanized sheet roofing of the hotel. Matheran is infested with monkeys, and we joked about it. In the evening we heard over the radio that a ship loaded with ammunition and TNT had exploded at the Bombay docks, causing widespread damage and destroying a part of the town. Being anxious about our home, we tried to get in touch with a friend, but the telephone lines were out of commission. After a few days, we returned to Bombay and found our home intact. We helped the people made homeless by the destruction.

With the approach of Indira's confinement, Feroze came to Bombay to be with her, for he had been released from prison a few days earlier. At about 5 A.M. on August 20 she woke us to say that she was having labor pains. I immediately telephoned Dr. Shirodkar to go to his nursing home and then we took Indira there. As it was her first child, she was afraid and wanted me to stay with her in the labor ward. I was very nervous myself, hoping and praying that all would go well. I harassed Dr. Shirodkar (as he told me later) by repeating over and over again, "Doctor, it has got to be a boy, because my brother has no son." It was a boy, born August 20, 1944, and we were all very happy. I sent Jawahar a telegram and wrote him a letter. As usual, the censors took their time, and the government delivered the letter and the telegram simultaneously.

Jawahar wrote:

I was happy to get the news—not so excited as you must have been, for excitement is less in my line. The birth of a new member of the family always makes one feel reminiscent and remember one's childhood days and other births. . . . And yet whenever a person arrives, it is something absolutely new, like others and still unique in its own way. Nature goes on repeating itself; there is no end to its infinite variety and every spring is a resurrection, every new birth a new beginning, especially when that new birth is intimately connected with us, it becomes a revival of ourselves and our old hopes center round it.

Dr. Shirodkar made fun of me for wanting a son for Indira while at my own confinement I had insisted that I wanted a girl. It was my second child, and since I already had a son, I very much wanted a daughter. Both my brother and sister had only daughters, and my mother, being old-fashioned, was disappointed. When my first son, Harsha, was born, she at last had a grandson. Not only Mother but also Jawahar, Nan, and dozens of other relatives rejoiced at his birth, congratulating me as if I had accomplished some tremendous feat. When my second son, Ajit, was born, my mother was angry with me for wanting a girl and not a boy. She had four granddaughters and thought it was high time she had a couple of grandsons.

Indira stayed with us for nearly two months after the birth of her son. As soon as she was strong enough to travel, she rejoined Feroze in their home in Lucknow—a home that was now blessed by the presence of their child. He was named Rajiv after his grandmother, for Rajiv and Kamala are both names of the lotus flower.

We had not seen Jawahar for more than two years, for visits from members of the family were now denied. Languishing in jail, he must have missed his family even more than we missed him. Personal contacts renew and revive the memories of loved faces and mutually shared experiences. In a letter to me he expressed his loneliness and isolation.

Meeting each other after a long interval shall we recognize each other in the old way? Or will there be a feeling of shyness and strangeness as when we meet those we do not fully understand? The private worlds each one of us lives in, worlds of fancy and feeling and imagination, have so long lain apart that they are apt to become strangers to each other, separate circles overlapping less than they used to. Partly that happens as we grow older, but the process is accelerated by the abnormal conditions we have been living in.

12

War's End

WITH THE ALLIES landing in France, the last phase of the European war had begun. In October, 1944, the government announced that the Ahmadnagar Fort prisoners would be allowed visits from their relatives. Nan and I applied for permission to visit Jawahar, but he had decided not to exercise the right of every prisoner which had been denied so long. He said that the conditions under which the interview was likely to take place were contrary to "my conception of my dignity and the dignity of my dear ones." In April, 1945, he was transferred to Bareilly (Uttar Pradesh) prison.

Toward the middle of April, Raja and I took a vacation in Kashmir where Indira and her son joined us. It was wonderful to be in our beautiful homeland. From Srinagar we went on a trekking trip way up in the mountains. Though we were cut off from all news, Raja felt that something important was happening and insisted on our returning to the valley. So we packed up our tents and started back to Pahalgam, the base of our trek. Pahalgam is generally full of tourists because of its wonderful climate, but we found that everybody was getting ready to leave for Srinagar. Somehow, with the help of a friend we got a car to take us to Srinagar. There we found confusion and excitement over the news of the release of all the political prisoners, including Jawahar, for Germany had surrendered on May 7.

Our joy at the defeat of Nazism was tinged with bitterness over the humiliation and inhuman separations that had been forced on our people in the name of freedom and democracy. I waited impatiently for news of my brother. A few days later we got his telegram: he was going to Bombay to see Gandhiji and then coming to Allahabad. We hurried to Allahabad to meet him. Indira and Feroze anxiously awaited him at Anand Bhawan. Once again we were all together. We were happy.

In June, 1945, Jawahar was summoned to a conference in Simla (Raja and I went with him), at which the Viceroy, Lord Wavell, would present a plan for the independence of India. Gandhiji, the Congress Working Committee, and Muslim League representatives had been invited.

Lord Wavell proposed a governing Executive Council composed of a majority of Indians. There were to be two British members (the Viceroy and the Commander in Chief), but all other members were to be Indians. Independence and democracy were still to be distant dreams. Any good that might have come out of the conference was undone by the demands of Mohammed Ali Jinnah, the president of the Muslim League, which I wrote about in *We Nehrus.*

The means Jinnah used to wreck the Simla Conference was to insist that he must name *all* the Muslims on the Viceroy's new Council. This, my brother and Gandhiji could not allow, because it would be a betrayal of all the good Muslims who had been loyal to the Congress party, including Maulana Azad, who was still its president. Though everyone, including Gandhiji and the Viceroy, tried hard to bring Jinnah to some compromise, he was as inflexible as an iceberg. After two weary weeks the conference broke up having accomplished exactly nothing.[1]

Though Lord Wavell may have tried sincerely to negotiate, his efforts were curbed by his advisers, the Government Services. The fact that only the Muslim League was invited to the conference as the representative of the Muslims doomed the negotiations from the outset. It ignored other Muslim organizations, which included the majority of Muslims in the country.

The proposed Executive Council made provision for giving equal representation to the Congress and the Muslim League. The Congress was a secular national organization and offered to nominate five members, including two Congress Muslims, to the proposed Council, but Jinnah refused to agree to the right of Congress to appoint any Muslim as a representative to the Council. He claimed that the Muslim League, as representative of all Muslims, alone could nominate them.

Jinnah and his Muslim League demanded the partition of India on the basis of religion—through the creation of a separate state of Pakistan out of predominantly Muslim areas of India. (The Pakistan concept had originated in the fertile brain of a British civil service officer in India.) Actually, Jinnah had little, if any, interest in religion. He was no Muslim, except perhaps by name. What he really wanted was to found a state in which he would be the great leader.

Great Britain once again used the divide-and-rule policy, which is characteristic of an imperial power in its treatment of a subject country. The British government of India did everything possible to fan the religious animosities and thus to strengthen the Muslim League. This gave rise to a Hindu-Muslim disunity, which afforded the British an excuse to stay in India. If Indians could not agree among themselves, there was no alternative but for Britain to continue to rule so that law and order could be preserved. At least, that was the self-righteous contention of the foreign ruler.

Then events took an unexpected turn in shaping the future of India. In England, the Churchill government was defeated when, on July 26, 1945, in a general election, the Labour party came to power, with Clement Attlee as Prime Minister. The Attlee government ordered elections in India to form a constitution-making body that would give India self-rule.

In India, the British could no longer rely on the loyalty of the armed forces. A major part of the Indian army in Singapore had joined the Indian National Liberation Army under Subhas Bose and fought the British. On February 19, 1946, the naval ratings in Bombay rose in mutiny at the treatment they received from their British officers and took possession of all the ships in the harbor. If Britain wanted to continue to govern India she would need considerable resources both in men and matériel, and at the end of the war (August, 1945) she could hardly afford them. Besides, the Labour government in Britain was psychologically prepared for an understanding with India.

So, in March, 1946, the British sent a "Cabinet Mission" to New Delhi to discuss with the Indian political parties the means of arriving at an agreement for the independence of India. But once again the proposals failed to meet the conflicting demands of the Congress, which was opposed to the partition of India, and the Muslim League. Ultimately the Cabinet Mission announced its own plan, under which an interim government was to be appointed and a constituent assembly convened to draft a constitution. The plan called for a federated Indian union: a central government with equal representation given to Muslims and Hindus.

The Working Committee of the Congress gave thoughtful consideration to the plan but accepted it only after Lord Wavell announced appointment of the Interim Government. The All-India Congress Committee held a meeting in Bombay on July 7 to ratify the plan. On August 12, Jawahar, as President of the Congress, was invited to form the Interim Government.

The Muslim League had accepted the plan in June, but almost immediately Jinnah regretted this action. And he regretted it all the more after the Indian National Congress ratified it. He withdrew the League's acceptance. At a July 27 meeting of the League he summoned its members to engage in a *jihad* ("holy war") against the Hindus. Under the spell of his fiery hate-rousing speech, the League passed a resolution for "direct action," and it set August 16 as Direct Action Day.

13

A Second Child

ALL THIS TIME Indira, her baby son Rajiv, and Feroze were at Anand Bhawan. Indira devoted herself to the care of her son, while Feroze made good use of the beautiful photographs he had taken in Europe to write for illustrated journals. He also worked at selling insurance. Under his care, the garden at Anand Bhawan bloomed with beautiful flowers, and it was a joy to see our home in its old glory.

In November, 1946, Feroze joined the *National Herald* in Lucknow as managing editor. Jawahar had founded this daily paper, published in English, in 1937, but he had since resigned from the board of directors. No doubt the idea to start a newspaper had come from our father who years ago had launched his own daily called *The Independent*, which had lasted only three years, ceasing publication when Father joined the Congress and could no longer afford it (it continued to lose large sums). In

1942, when the Quit India movement started, the *National Herald* also had to suspend publication, for it refused to submit to censorship. The paper resumed publication in November, 1946, so Feroze and his family moved to Lucknow.

In Lucknow, Feroze took a small house and furnished it with great care. He designed his own furniture and again applied his love of gardening. He worked all day and often long hours to put the *National Herald* on its feet. The paper had always been in financial difficulties, but with Feroze in charge, it almost became self-supporting. He wisely used the idle capacity of the press by taking on miscellaneous printing jobs. The editor of the paper spoke of Feroze as "a man with the common touch" who worked day and night, loved machines, and endeared himself to the workers.

Indira busied herself with housekeeping and with local Congress activities and social welfare work. Both Feroze and Indira had progressive socialist views, and many young politicians frequented their home, but they were very different in character—she shy and reserved and he more outgoing and informal. Life in their little home in Lucknow may not have been quite what Indira had been used to in Anand Bhawan, but she and Feroze shared love and affection and desire to understand and help each other.

As interim Prime Minister, Jawahar had to have an official residence in New Delhi. He took a small house at 17 York Road. Besides his own suite, it had a large drawing room, rooms for members of his family, and working quarters for his staff. In the process of setting up the house, Indira and I shuttled to and fro between New

Delhi and our homes in Lucknow and Bombay. Indira
came from Lucknow as often as possible to be her father's
helpmate, but because she was expecting her second
child, Nan and I often acted as hostesses. Indira was to
have her confinement in New Delhi, since the capital city
offered better medical facilities than Lucknow.

Raja and I were preparing to go to the United States
early in January, 1947, for our first lecture tour, but before our departure I wanted to be with Jawahar and
Indira, so I went there in December. Indira was somewhat unhappy about my plans for leaving before the
arrival of her baby, especially because I had been with
her when her first child was born. The day before my
return to Bombay, her doctor came to examine her. He
told me that there were still three weeks to go and that
"she is very upset at the idea of your leaving tomorrow." I
would have gladly postponed my departure for the States,
but he assured me that there would not be much difficulty, since it was her second baby.

That evening we all gathered for a family dinner—
Jawahar, Indira, Feroze, who had come from Lucknow,
and my two sons, who were home for holidays from
Scindia School. We had a pleasant evening. Jawahar's wit-
ticisms brought a great deal of laughter, and Indira was in
fine form. The next morning, at about 3 A.M., Indira's
maid woke me to say that Indira was having labor pains. I
could not believe it; perhaps her subconscious desire for
my presence at the birth brought on the labor. Feroze and
I, without waking Jawahar, took her to the hospital and
called her doctor. He showed annoyance at being called
so early, and he did not allow me to be with Indira in the
labor ward. We walked up and down the cold corridors.

After what seemed like hours, the doctor came out and told us that Indira had a bad time, that she had lost a lot of blood, and that he had "saved her." Was it a boy? a girl? He didn't bother to tell us. As soon as we learned from the nurses that Indira had given birth to a son, we rang up Jawahar, who hurried over to the hospital. He was alarmed at seeing his daughter so weak, so white and bloodless.

Indira chose the name Sanjay for her second son. Before I left Bombay for the lecture tour, she wrote me from the hospital:

Darling Chitti,
I always seem to be saying thank you to you. And it is such an inadequate way of expressing what I really want to say. I wish I could do something for you in return. I'm not a bit satisfied with your "daughter" complex.

However, it was really the greatest bit of luck for me that you were here when the baby arrived. I was quite dreading being all alone on the occasion. . . . The wonderful thing about you is that you have always appeared whenever I have wanted somebody to stand by. Not once but so many times.

A second letter came two days later via Raja. He had gone to Delhi at the request of Jawahar, who wished to offer him the post of India's high commissioner in Malaya. Raja refused the post, for he felt that the real work for years to come was in India and not in Indian embassies abroad. Indira wrote:

I have a special feeling for you which has nothing to do with your being my aunt. I still remember how I used to admire and worship you as a kid, and my love for you has grown and not diminished with the years. All that you have done for me and my babies has forged a special tie between us that I hope will get stronger as time goes by.

I needed no thanks from Indira. I have loved her as my daughter. I treasure these letters. They have meant much to me.

14

Partition of India and the Hindu-Muslim Struggle

HARDLY HAD JAWAHAR accepted the Viceroy's invitation to form a government, when bloody riots broke out in Calcutta on the sixteenth of August, 1946, the "Direct Action Day" fixed by the Muslim League. A few days earlier Jinnah had stated, "We have forged a pistol and are in a position to use it to achieve Pakistan." Bengal had a Muslim League ministry in office, and the provincial government stood aside while people ran amuck committing murder, rape, and arson. Jinnah and the League fanned mob violence against the Hindus, which in turn led to bitter reprisals by the Hindus against the Muslims.

In 1946, the British government had not yet abdicated its authority over India, and "law and order" was its special duty as the ruler of the country. The inhuman riots suited the British policy of dividing the country. This is no apology for our people, for their disgrace is undeniable, but it must be remembered that the British have never left any colony without partitioning it—as in the case of Ireland and finally India—usually resulting in chaos and a means to maintain a foothold in the country.

And so the massacre continued. From Calcutta to East Bengal, from Noakhali to Bihar to the cities in northern India, the fire ignited by the vainglorious pride of one man and the ebbing tide of an empire consumed innocent men, women, and children in its wake. There was not one Nero who fiddled while Rome burned, but two, Jinnah and the Viceroy, who did not raise one finger in horror to stop the carnage.

Gandhiji, the apostle of nonviolence and truth, rushed from one village to another to put out the fire with his message of love and friendship between Hindus and Muslims, only to find that the fire had been lit in yet another place. At this distant time it is difficult for others to understand the anguish of our hearts when we found friends had become enemies overnight for no reason at all. As Gandhiji walked barefoot from village to village, Tagore's famous song expressed the anguish in his heart.

Walk alone
If they answer not to thy call, walk alone;
If they are afraid and cower mutely facing the wall
O thou of evil luck,
Open thy mind and speak out alone.
If they turn away and desert you when crossing the
wilderness
O thou of evil luck,
Trample the thorns under thy tread,
And along the blood-lined track, travel alone.

If they do not hold up the light when the night is
   troubled with storm,
O thou of evil luck,
With the thunder-flame of pain ignite thine own
   heart
And let it burn alone.

Jawahar, at great risk to himself, toured the devastated
areas to calm the people and instill courage. In the midst
of all the turbulence, the Muslim League decided to join
the Interim Government in order to fight the Congress
from within. In this move, the League was aided by the
senior officials of the British government of India. Jawahar
charged the Viceroy, Lord Wavell, with "removing the
wheels of the car" (that is, government). Early in 1947,
Lord Wavell was replaced by Lord Mountbatten, and the
Attlee government declared its decision to withdraw from
India by June, 1948.

On June 3, 1947, Lord Mountbatten announced the
plan for the partition of India. Our country was to be
divided into the Indian Union and Pakistan. The Indian
Union was to consist of a predominantly Hindu population, and Pakistan of a predominantly Muslim population.

Naturally, the Muslim League, which had been agitat-
ing for partition, accepted the plan at once. The Congress,
under the leadership of Jawahar and Sardar Vallabhbhai,
convinced that the alternatives were anarchy or partition,
resigned itself to accepting partition for the sake of peace
and independence. Gandhiji alone persisted in standing
out against it. He wrote, "All it [the British government]
has to do is to withdraw and leave India . . . maybe even in
chaos, on or before the promised date." The acceptance of
partition, he said, amounted to acknowledging "that

everything was to be got if mad violence was perpetrated in sufficient measure."

On July 18, British rule was given up by act of Parliament, to be effective on August 15, 1947.

On the evening of August 14, mammoth crowds gathered on the streets throughout the country to usher in India's independence. The long struggle for freedom, which had claimed so many sacrifices and so much suffering, had come to an end. On Independence Day, August 15, we were excited and proud that we had taken part in the struggle. For years we had thought of nothing but working in the cause of freedom, and we had never dreamt that this day would come in our lifetime. Jawahar, addressing the Assembly in New Delhi, said: "Long years ago we made a tryst with destiny, and now the time comes when we shall redeem our pledge, not wholly or in full measure but very substantially." Now India was free from British rule.

At the same time, our hearts were sad. Independence had been won, but our country was partitioned and religious frenzy had been let loose. To us Nehrus, who had been brought up in an atmosphere of agnosticism and who made no distinction between peoples on the ground of religion, the fighting between adherents of rival religions was incomprehensible and horrifying.

Muslims had been an integral part of India for hundreds of years. They were our own people, racially and otherwise. We had a common history. Indian culture was a synthesis of Hinduism and the Islam. We had absorbed the traditions of our Muslim invaders. Some of the Hindus accepted Islam as their faith, but the majority remained in the Hindu fold. Yet when the Muslim League and

Mohammed Ali Jinnah—himself a Hindu by only one generation—called for a *jihad* against erstwhile brothers, the illiterate masses of India fell upon each other, and even the more educated joined in the religious conflict. Many of our friends left their ancestral homes for Pakistan in the hope of securing a better future. But the millions who went to Pakistan and the millions who came to India were refugees and lost everything. However, India affirmed that she was a secular state, and millions of Muslims did stay on in India. Jawahar and his government did everything possible to protect them without discrimination.

Hardly had the celebrations of August 15 ended when the news of a new massacre in Punjab, involving five million Hindus and Sikh refugees, ignited riots in New Delhi. Jawahar, without fear for his own safety, toured the turbulent areas to pacify the people and protect the Muslims. He was terribly distressed. Unflinchingly he condemned the atrocities and urged the people to behave like human beings and not savages. He helped to transfer the Muslim population to well-protected areas, where camps were put up for them, and he opened his own home to house some of the refugees.

The Punjab massacre rekindled hatreds in Calcutta. Gandhiji, who was in Calcutta, was attacked by an angry Hindu mob. On September 1 he announced another fast unto death, hoping that it would bring peace between the Hindu and Muslim communities. "What my word in person cannot do," he said, "my fast may." He declared that he would break his fast if the Hindu-Muslim killings were to stop. His fast achieved a miracle: the two communities pledged their word to keep the peace.

Gandhiji came to Delhi on September 9, 1947, and found the city paralyzed by riots. Jawahar and his government had taken stern measures against violence, but Gandhiji was not happy with the restrictions imposed by the police and the military. He wanted the conversion of the hearts of the people. To bring this about, he stayed on in Delhi. One day I was among a group of young men and women visiting him. He had undertaken yet another fast, to protest the bitterness and violence in Delhi, where even the life of Maulana Azad, the veteran Congress leader, was not safe. He told us that every Indian patriot worthy of his name should work for the unity of the people of India. Indira and all of us took the pledge to work toward this end.

Indira, who had remained anemic after the birth of her second son, was still not well, but she rallied for the work of alleviating the misery of the refugees. She could not bear to see the sorrow on her father's face, and was spurred to relieve him of some of his duties. Having made arrangements for the care of her children, she went to the refugee camps, where she calmed the bitterness in the hearts of people and tried to lighten their hardships. The refugees responded to the sympathy and help they got from the daughter of Jawahar.

When news of fresh violence toward Hindus came from Pakistan, a new wave of violence broke out in Delhi. A mob surrounded the house of a poor Muslim, threatening to kill everybody inside. As soon as Indira heard this, she went to the Muslim house. On their arrival, there were no guards or police to protect them. The mob shouted abuses and threats at Indira, but she pushed her way through the crowd and went into the house, where she found the family cowering with fear of their lives. She told them not to be afraid and to follow her. While the angry Hindus hurled insults at her (somehow they did not dare to stop her), she got the whole Muslim family into her jeep and took them to her father's house.

Gradually the violence subsided and sanity returned. Gandhiji accepted the pledges of the leaders of the opposing communities to keep the peace, and he gave up his fast.

In January, 1948, I was once again in Delhi, at the invitation of my brother. I was not feeling well, and he thought the cool climate would be good for me. I wanted to see Gandhiji, and his secretary arranged for a visit on January 29. It was scheduled for noon, when there would be no visitors except for our group. Indira, her son Rajiv, Padmaja Naidu, and I went at the appointed hour. We found Gandhiji sitting in the garden having his midday meal of mashed vegetables. He was wearing a Noakhali peasant straw hat, and as we greeted him he smiled and said, "What do you think of my hat? Don't I look handsome in it?" We laughed and sat down around him. He asked each of us what we were doing and inquired about our families. He looked extremely fit after his fast, and his bare body glowed with health. Indira's four-year-old son Rajiv kept twining flowers round his feet. Bapu pulled Rajiv's ears lovingly and said, "Don't you know one does not put flowers around the feet of one who is alive?" Rajiv was too young to understand, but I quickly took the flowers away.

When it came time to leave, I hesitated and lingered behind the others. Gandhiji asked if I had something special to say to him. I said that I wanted to come again to see him when no one else was there. He pulled me down affectionately to sit by his side, embraced me, and said, "So many people want to see me. How can I refuse them? Perhaps the next time you will have to see me with crowds." Little did I know that that was to be my last visit with Bapu, the last glimpse of his dearly loved face.

The next day, on January 30, Mahatma Gandhi was slain. As he stood up to speak to the assembled crowd at a prayer meeting, a young Hindu fired three shots into his body.

The news of Gandhiji's death stunned the country. Verily, the light had gone out. But the bullet that killed Gandhiji pierced the hearts of millions and killed the communal hatred that had possessed them.

After the ceremony of the immersion of Gandhi's ashes in the waters of the Ganges, Jawahar addressed the great gathering. It was a long speech. He said, in part:

In his life as in his death there has been a radiance which will illumine our country for ages to come. Why then should we grieve for him? Let us grieve rather for ourselves, for our own weakness, for the ill will in our hearts, for our dissensions and for our conflicts. Remember that it was to remove all these that Mahatmaji gave his life. Remember that during the past few months it was on this that he concentrated his vast energy and service. . . .

Our country gave birth to a mighty one and he shone like a beacon not only for India but for the whole world. . . .

Throughout his life he thought of India in terms of the poor and the oppressed and the downtrodden. To raise them and free them was the mission of his life. He adopted their ways of life and dress so that none in the country may feel lowly. Victory to him was the growth of freedom of these people.[1]

15

A New Era for India

THE FIRST TIME Jawahar attended a meeting of Commonwealth prime ministers—in September, 1948—he had private talks with Prime Minister Attlee, but India was not a subject of discussion at the official gathering of heads of state. At the next meeting of prime ministers, held in London in April, 1949, Jawahar proposed "that India remain in the Commonwealth provided she could do so as a sovereign independent republic, with no strings attached and no oath of allegiance to the Crown." The proposal confounded the British Foreign Office lawyers. They asked, "How could you have a republic in an organization that owed allegiance to the King?"[1]

Under pressure from Prime Minister Attlee and King George VI, the British "finally worked out a formula. The Declaration of London stated that while the other members of the Commonwealth remained united by their common *allegiance* to the Crown, India became a full member simply by . . . 'her acceptance of the King, as the symbol of the free association of its independent member nations and as such the Head of the Commonwealth.' Thus the British actually altered the principle of membership in the Commonwealth in order to admit India."[2]

India was to become a republic in a matter of months, but before that happened the Constituent Assembly, in which the Congress party had the majority, was engaged in angry debates. While the constitution of India was being framed by the Assembly, there were stormy pro and con arguments on every suggested provision—the question of a national language, the form of parliamentary government, the bill of rights (with a provision against untouchability). However, Jawahar's opinions carried weight, and the majority of Congress supported his views.

The conflict within the Congress had both an organizational and an ideological basis. To begin with, it had been a loosely knit organization fashioned to wage the struggle against the British government in India. Its only unifying force had been the national will to freedom. Communists, socialists, and conservatives alike worked for the common goal. Even Jawahar's Fabian socialist ideas on economic and social questions were acceptable to the Congress as long as they were only an exercise in political daydreaming. But once freedom had been achieved, conflicts between various groups within the Congress emerged. In 1947, Gandhi had actually advised that the Congress be dissolved and that new political parties be formed, but Jawahar and Sardar Vallabhbhai (his colleague in the Congress) did not agree with Gandhi's views on dissolution.

The Constituent Assembly met from 1947 to 1948, and on November 26, 1949, the constitution of India, establishing a republic, was adopted. It provided for universal suffrage, a bicameral parliament, a prime minister, and a bill of rights. It also provided for Hindi as the official language and English as an associate language of the Central Legislature.

India became a sovereign republic—the Republic of India—and a member of the British Commonwealth of Nations on January 26, 1950.

In October, 1949, Jawahar and Indira made their first trip to the United States. Jawahar had been invited as a guest of President Truman, and he was to fly from London on the President's plane. This happened to be the very time when Raja and I were going to America on our second lecture tour. With our two sons, I left India for the States ten days ahead of Jawahar and Indira. Raja was to follow much later. After stopping in Egypt for a few days, we joined Jawahar and Indira on the Air-India plane from Cairo to London. In London, I asked Jawahar if I could fly with him on the President's plane, but he said it would be against protocol. So the rest of us flew by regular airline.

My children and I were with Jawahar and Indira in between their official engagements and at breakfast whenever they were in New York. Indira did not attend all the official functions to which Jawahar was invited, so she and I went window shopping, to lunches with my friends, and to museums and art galleries. One of my friends invited us to a nightclub. Indira does not take part in social dancing, and though I love dancing we just had a supper, watched the floor show, and then went home. Indira loves the theater and saw several plays. She enjoyed the visit and made many friends in the States. Being keenly observant, she has the ability to retain a distinct memory of the people and scenes of a foreign country. She found the Americans "a lovable people," but their lavish hospitality was a bit too much for her. Since this first visit she has often been to the States.

The official residence of the Prime Minister at 17 York Road was too small for the transaction of government business and ceremonial affairs. The constant flow of guests who came for a brief stay and sometimes a long stay, the visits of members of the family, and the many people who came on various errands necessitated a larger residence. Besides, security was difficult, since the house was almost on the road. Jawahar did not worry about his personal security, but he did need privacy for his work in addition to space for all the official activities. Lord Mountbatten suggested his moving to the house that had served as residence for the British commander in chief—a large house of great splendor with spacious rooms and a beautiful garden. At first Jawahar was reluctant, because he did not like to be cut off from contact with the people and live in isolation, but he finally agreed. The place came to be known as the Prime Minister's House. (It is now called Teen Murti House.)

When, in 1950, Indira set up the new house for her father, neither he nor she thought that she would make it her permanent home. At first she often took the children to Lucknow to spend a few days with Feroze. But as Jawahar's burden of office increased and the tension in the

1. Indira with her mother, Kamala

2. *Motilal Nehru, circa 1907*

3. *Young Jawaharlal Nehru* (standing) *and his father, M(*

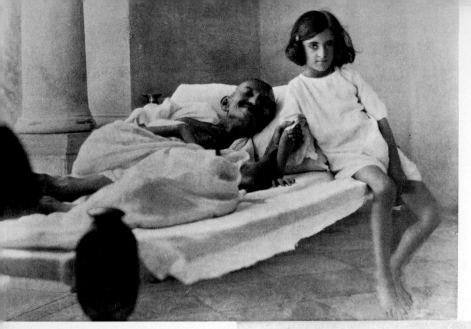

4. *Gandhi and Indira*

5. *Indira at school
in Poona*

6. Nehru, Indira (right), *and his sisters Mme. Krishna Nehru Hutheesing* (extreme left) *and Mme. Pandit. Next to Mme. Pandit is her daughter, Lekha.*
Photo courtesy of P. N. Sharma

7. *Swaraj Bhawan*

9. *Indira and Ne*

8. *Indira Gandhi taking the oath of office as Prime Minister of India in 1966*

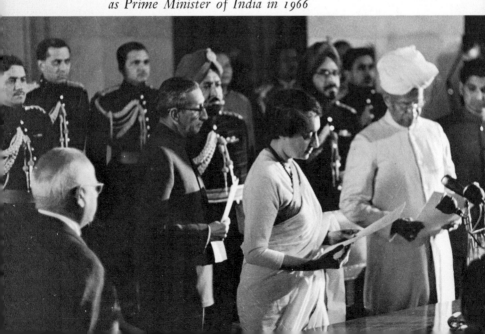

10. *One of the last pictures of Krishna Nehru Hutheesing.*
Photo courtesy of the Cincinnati *Enquirer*

country continued, it seemed essential for her to remain in New Delhi, not only to act as hostess when important visitors came from abroad but also to manage the household and see to her father's comforts. As his daughter, this was her rightful place. My sister was always abroad on a diplomatic assignment, and I was living in Bombay, where my husband and children needed me. Even so, I often went to Delhi. Feroze, realizing that Indira should be with her father during these crucial days, suggested that instead of her traveling the 270 miles to Lucknow with the children from time to time, he would make frequent visits to Delhi.

After the partition of India, Jawahar received threatening letters against his life. The protection of his person continued to be a vital need. Indira did not have an easy time acting as watchdog—keeping political opportunists, visitors who had no set purpose, and just busybodies out of his way. This called for tact and delicate handling of people. In addition she carried on social welfare work and was a member of Congress subcommittees. But she never allowed any of these activites to interfere with her relation to her children.

Indira was a tender mother, who gave as much time as possible to the rearing of her two sons, Rajiv and Sanjay. Remembering her own loneliness as a child, she wanted them to have a normal childhood. She supervised their meals, played with them, and took them to a film if a suitable one for children was being shown. The boys were secure in their mother's affection. But since they were at an age when they needed constant attention, she summoned Anna (a Dane who had made India her home) to aid her. Anna had been a secretary to J. C. Bose, a famous scientist, and subsequently the governess of Nan's daughters. She was a strict disciplinarian, an ardent believer in cold showers, sunbathing, and exercise, and a vegetarian, sometimes subsisting on a diet of raw vegetables and yogurt. When Rajav and Sanjay were enrolled in the Welham School in Dehra Dun, she took over the management of the household, thus relieving Indira of tiresome tasks.

Feroze, too, was a devoted parent. He constructed toys for his sons and interested them in finding out how machines worked and how to take things apart and put them together again. He wanted them to become engineers. (He was so successful in inculcating an interest in mechanical structures and processes that both sons chose the profession of engineering in adulthood.)

The death of several of Jawahar's colleagues in the Congress—men who had cooperated with him in trying to solve the problems of India—gave him a feeling of fighting battles alone. Among those who died were Govind Vallabh Pant, Sardar Vallabhbhai, and Rafi Ahmad Kidwai. Some of his colleagues in the Congress seemed to lack a vision of the world of tomorrow. And so Jawahar often sought council from Indira. Having been an observer at diplomatic conversations concerned with negotiations, both at home and abroad, she had a clear understanding of historical developments, and Jawahar trusted her judgment.

Indira's extensive knowledge of history had begun when, on her thirteenth birthday, her father (from Naini prison) wrote her the first of the letters that were later published as *Glimpses of World History*. Now she was truly participating in a living history. She accompanied her father on his various historical missions to foreign countries: in 1948 and 1949 to the meetings of the Commonwealth prime ministers in London, and then to Paris, where he addressed the General Assembly of the United Nations on India's foreign policy, relating it to the aspirations of Asian and African peoples; in 1953 to London for the coronation of Queen Elizabeth; in 1954 on Jawahar's official visit to China; and in 1955 to the Afro-Asian Conference held in Bandung, Indonesia, where Jawahar, as spokesman for the Afro-Asian bloc, tried to bring China into the comity of Afro-Asian nations, hoping that amelioration of international relations would influence Chinese extremism.

On her return from England in 1953, Indira visited Soviet Russia in a private capacity. This visit gave her perspectives on Russian life and government, and her visit to China the following year enabled her to compare political and social conditions in the two Communist countries. Privately, she voiced apprehensions about China's intentions toward India and Southeast Asia. Her views differed from those of Jawahar, who, in 1954, invited Chou En-lai to India as a state guest. Their meetings resulted in the declaration of *Pancha Shila*, which proclaimed five principles of friendship to be mutually observed by the two nations: respect for the other's territory and sovereignty; nonaggression; noninterference with internal affairs; equality and mutual benefits; and peaceful coexistence.

Jawahar believed that China would abide by her pledges, because, he said, these two great civilizations "had lived at peace with each other for a thousand years, neither country playing the role of aggressor, but both having intimate cultural and commercial contacts throughout these ages."[3]

Many foreign dignitaries, attracted by Jawaharlal Nehru's vigorous work for Indian independence and by his concern for international amity, came to Delhi—among them, Khrushchev, Bulganin, Nassar, Chou En-lai, and Eleanor Roosevelt. For Indira it was an opportunity to make the acquaintance of eminent people from all over the globe and to keep abreast of transactions of great importance, for she was present as an observer at meetings where unsettled matters affecting the whole world were discussed.

Inside and outside the country, Jawahar had to deal with momentous problems. Since Pakistan invaded Kashmir in 1947, the relations between India and Pakistan had steadily deteriorated. When Pakistan was established in 1947, it comprised two major areas—East Pakistan and West Pakistan, separated by nine hundred miles of the north-central part of India—and Pakistan needed to unify its diverse peoples. India followed a policy aimed at the betterment of her people, but in Pakistan the big *zamindars* (landowners) exploited the masses and amassed vast fortunes. The Pakistani government felt obliged to divert the attention of the peasantry away from the inequities of life, and religion provided the instrument. The Kashmir dispute was brought before the United Nations in 1948, and a cease-fire was effected in 1949. But the dispute has continued to the present day.

At home, Jawahar faced dissension among various

groups, but he effectively presented programs of development objectives. He believed in a welfare state of a socialist pattern, to be achieved by consent of the people and not by coercion. He laid great stress on planning, which alone could raise standards of living for the common man and make his latent talents useful. Planning implied state regulation and controls. He favored state enterprise for the country's economic development. Through his influence, five-year plans were instituted and vast industrial and agricultural projects undertaken. He personally visited the sites considered for new projects and took time to preside at cornerstone-laying ceremonies. Gradually his policies brought about better use of national resources and the country's growth in economic development.

Indira, too, visited the projects, and she saw how they were transforming the country. The continuing planning process and the expansion in agriculture and industry were a token of her father's faith in India's destiny—and they inspired her to strive for the ideals her father worked for.

The first general elections under the new constitution were held in 1952. The Congress campaign centered round the love the people of India had for Jawahar. He was their idol, for he was improving their lot in life. No matter who the local candidate was, Congress posters announced, "A vote for Congress is a vote for Nehru." Jawahar traveled the length and breadth of the land—by plane, car, train, and bullock cart. Often Indira campaigned alongside him. Sometimes a local candidate would take her to his constituency in support of his ticket, and she found that she could move crowds and influence them.

Even before the 1952 elections, the State Congress Committee of Uttar Pradesh had asked her to stand for election to the state legislature, but she refused because she wanted to devote herself to her children and to social welfare work. She had fostered the establishment of organizations for the development of Indian music and dance and of Indian films, especially for children. She was the president of the Indian Council of Child Welfare and a member of the Central Social Welfare Board of the Government of India. Politics could wait while these activities demanded her attention. Besides, Jawahar needed her as hostess and as consultant when perplexing problems came up.

So Indira made her home in her father's house in Delhi. In the process she had to sacrifice her family life with Feroze. It has been said that Feroze was unhappy and that he thought Indira preferred the limelight of life in the Prime Minister's House to the anonymity of being the wife of a private individual. I know this is not true. Indira once wrote to me, "And you know his [Jawahar's] habit of giving last place to the members of his family. . . . When he is in the midst of any work, he always puts aside all personal feelings and obligations." I am sure Feroze understood this.

16

Separate Careers; Feroze's Death

IN THE GENERAL ELECTIONS of 1952, Feroze stood as a Congress candidate from Bareilly for the Lok Sabha (the lower house of the Central Legislature). Elected by a big majority, he resigned as managing editor of the *National Herald* and moved to New Delhi, where he joined his wife and children in a suite in the Prime Minister's House. As a member of the Parliament, he was allotted a house of his own, which he maintained as a separate dwelling for himself, since he had to have an office for receiving his visitors and space to entertain his guests. Having brought the furniture of his own design from Lucknow, he decorated the rooms attractively. The house had a small garden, and he could once more indulge his passion for floriculture.

Feroze was very attached to Rafi Ahmed Kidwai, the Minister for Food and Agriculture, with whom he had worked for the *National Herald*. Rafi Saheb was once secretary to my father and later became the most able organizer of the Congress movement in U.P. Jawahar relied on him and believed in his abilities as an organizer and efficient administrator. As a minister in the Central Cabinet, Rafi Saheb showed his capacity to get the work done and successfully helped the country to overcome its food problem as long as he lived to be in charge of the ministry. Though he believed in a socialist pattern of society, he suffered from no rigid dogma and used private businessmen as well as public service men for the work he undertook.

Feroze learned much through his friendship with Rafi Saheb and like him was easily accessible and always ready to help poor people. Cab drivers, postmen, railway porters, and hawkers came to him with their problems, and he willingly took up their cause. It was therefore necessary for him to have his house open to everyone. At the Prime Minister's House, security restrictions would have precluded Feroze's maintaining an open house.

Feroze was proud. He disliked being introduced as the son-in-law of the Prime Minister and avoided being photographed with his father-in-law, for his sense of personal worth demanded that he be known as an individual and not as an appendage to the Nehru family. He also avoided social functions if he was invited as a son-in-law, and attended only those functions to which he was invited as a member of Parliament.

Raja and I were genuinely fond of him, as he was of us. Whenever I was in New Delhi, he would drop into my room mornings after breakfast for a talk. Raja used to tease him about being "the nation's son-in-law," and Feroze would make a retort about "the nation's brother-in-law."

Much was made of Feroze's separate house, with its implications of a rift between him and Indira. Even in the Parliament it was rumored that the provision in the Hindu Marriage Bill to facilitate divorce was promoted in order to enable Indira to get a divorce. People forget that Indira and Feroze did not need to go through any divorce proceedings and, moreover, they truely loved each other. But to this day writers continue to play up the unhappiness of the marriage.

In 1966, Indira made a statement to an interviewer to set things straight:

> I hear these stories that my marriage collapsed and I left my husband, or that we were separated, and it's not true. It wasn't an ideally happy marriage. We were very happy at times. We quarreled tremendously at times. It was partly because both of us were so headstrong, and partly circumstances. I wouldn't have gone into public life if he had said no. But I am so intense in whatever I do, he must have been frightened to have it all concentrated on him. He wanted me occupied. He was very occupied with his own career. But when I went into public life and became successful, he liked it and he didn't like it. Other people—friends, relatives—were the worst. They would say, "How does it feel, being so-and-so's husband?" He would get upset, and it would take me weeks to win him over. To hurt the male ego is, of course, the biggest sin in marriage. . . . Toward the end, we were somehow getting beyond all this and becoming very close.[1]

Both were motivated by dedication to India's advancement, and both gave their best to their country. As a freshman member of Parliament, Feroze assumed a minor role in the deliberations of the Lok Sabha, but he made a determined effort to become familiar with the parliamentary system of government and to become an expert on procedures and rules. Before making his first speech, he prepared his case with meticulous care. The subject of this speech was the misuse of funds by an insurance company—the Bharat Insurance Company, one of the enterprises of the big Dalmia-Jain group of industries. His exposé of shady business dealings led to the appointment of a commission of inquiry, to the conviction of Rama Krishna Dalmia and ultimately to the nationalization of the life insurance business. His presentation of the case gave him a reputation of being unafraid to speak his mind, even if it meant exposing important personages.

In the general elections of 1957, Feroze was returned to the Lok Sabha, and he again showed that he was a fearless crusader. He brought allegations against the Finance Ministry, which had sanctioned a big loan to a businessman, Haridas Mundra, by the nationalized Life Insurance Corporation. The then Finance Minister, T. T. Krishnamachari, was one of the ablest ministers of the government of India, and Jawahar was upset at the charges but agreed to a judicial inquiry by Chief Justice Chagla of the Bombay High Court. (Chagla later became Indian ambassador to the United States, and subsequently Minister for External Affairs.) Feroze, the chief witness, brought a wealth of detail before the court. The report of the inquiry was an embarrassment to Jawahar, for it implicated a colleague and high officials of the government. Nevertheless, he engaged in a campaign deploring the conduct of the officials involved and demanding punishment. The Finance Minister resigned. Feroze, who was himself unhappy about the affair, is said to have remarked, *"Array, Kahan mara, kahan laga?"* ("Oh where did I aim, and where did I hit?"). The inquiry created a tremendous stir and received world-wide publicity.

Thus Feroze made a name for himself as a member of Parliament. He was a good speaker, an able administrator, and a fearless champion of worthy causes.

Because of his extraordinarily appealing qualities, he had many friends, whom he sometimes amused by playing pranks on them. But more often he performed good deeds —such as finding the right husband for girls who had no way of meeting eligible men. He rather liked being a matchmaker. At parties for children he was great fun.

There is no doubt that his reactions to life at the Prime Minister's House were due in part to his background, which was so different from Indira's. He came from a middle-class Parsi family of modest means. The funds for his education in England had been provided by an aunt, a successful doctor in Lucknow, who was very fond of him. He may have felt ill at ease in the midst of social formalities. Such unimportant things as the order of precedence laid down by protocol became a complex with him. In 1958 he decided to live alone, and moved to his own house. But he continued to have daily meals with Indira and the children at the Prime Minister's House.

Soon after having moved, he had a heart attack. Indira was on a political mission to Nepal. A long-distance call was put through, and she left immediately for Delhi. She nursed her husband devotedly, and he recovered quickly. Then Feroze, Indira, and their children went to Kashmir for its wonderful climate. There they found relaxation and recreation. In Indira's words, "We had a nearly perfect holiday."[2] On their return, Feroze once again plunged into work.

On September 2, 1960, Feroze complained of a pain in his chest. Instead of following his doctor's advice to take a rest, he attended the Lok Sabha sessions. Five days later, he phoned his doctor for a consultation, got into his car, and drove alone to the nursing·home, where he collapsed with a second heart attack. Indira, who was reached in Kerala in the south, made a fast return trip to Delhi. Feroze's condition worsened during the night, while Indira kept vigil by his bedside. In the early hours of the morning of September 8, Feroze died holding Indira's hand.

Rajiv and Sanjay came home from their school in Dehra Dun. Raja and I went to Delhi but arrived too late for the funeral. Feroze, though he was a Parsi (Parsis take their dead to the Tower of Silence or bury them), had expressed a wish to be cremated, and so his body was taken to the cremation grounds and the funeral pyre was lit by his son Rajiv. Thousands of laborers and poor people whom he had helped followed the funeral procession.

Indira was heartbroken. She locked herself in her room. Realizing that she wanted to be alone with her grief, I went to my brother's room. He was sitting gazing into space, quite stunned and unaware of his surroundings. As I put my arms around him, he said with a choking voice, "It happened so quickly. He was so young and, I did not know, so popular. He kept asking for Indu."

17

Indira Goes
on Fact-Finding Tours

TRAVELING THROUGHOUT INDIA became, for a time, Indira's chief occupational activity. The Congress Working Committee, to which she was appointed in 1955, put her in charge of the Women's Department, which meant that she had to traverse the country to organize local units of women and promote the understanding of Congress policies.

In the 1957 general elections she campaigned for Jawahar in Phulpur, where she visited practically every village of the 1,100-village rural constituency. Her speeches drew great crowds, and her mingling freely with the people won popular affection for her. She also campaigned in Gujarat, where there were demonstrations and mob violence. Its people were demanding separation from the state of Bombay, which comprised Maharashtra and Gujarat.

Within the Congress there were opposing forces on the question of authority for policies. Should the Prime Minister lay down policies to be followed by the Congress party? Or should the Congress organization lay down the policies? Before the era of independence, the President of the Congress had the position and powers of the leader, but after independence he was often a mere figurehead and the Prime Minister was the leader. The conflict led to the resignation of two Congress presidents. From 1951 to 1954, Jawahar, in addition to being Prime Minister, was again President of the Congress. From 1955 to 1958, U. N. Dhebar held the office of president. By then the Congress had lost its importance as a mass organization. From then on it was the party in the legislatures that took over the role of laying down policies.

Early in 1959, leftist elements in the Congress formed what they called the "Ginger Group." They pressed for implementation of Jawahar's socialist program, but the rightists prevented implementation by delaying tactics. The Ginger Group (both Indira and Feroze had joined it) was short-lived.

In February, 1959, Indira was elected President of the Congress. Some said that Jawahar was responsible for elevating her to the presidency. This was untrue, for he firmly believed that a position should be earned by reason of merit, and not by reason of relationship. Indira was the fourth woman to head the party, so it was nothing new. She quickly proved her ability when she undertook a tour to one of the southernmost states of India—to the state of Kerala, bordering on the Arabian Sea.

This was a tour of investigation of a situation embroiled in political complications. Indira wanted to see things for herself. In 1957, Kerala had elected a Communist government, which provoked nationwide concern. It had the largest percentage of literacy of any state in India and consequently a greater degree of unemployment among the educated. Roman Catholic clergy dominated the life of the Roman Catholics, who formed a strong minority of the people. Though the Communists had won power under a democratic constitution, they subverted this power by putting party men in administrative agencies and police services, by misusing public funds for party purposes, by failing to uphold law and order, and by interfering with the judiciary. They began the indoctrination of school children by rewriting textbooks, and they abolished denominational schools. Not only the Roman Catholics but also other religious groups were aroused, but the Communist ministry suppressed all protests and peaceful demonstrations. Yet the government of India hesitated to remove a ministry duly elected by the voters.

It was Indira Gandhi's penetrating analysis, based on her journey through Kerala, that ultimately resulted in a beneficent change. On her return to Delhi she persuaded the Central Legislature to dismiss the Communist ministry of Kerala and to put the state under the President's rule. A provision of the constitution of India gave the President such emergency powers. Fresh elections were ordered. Indira once more wandered through Kerala, from end to end—this time to campaign. The state Congress party was returned to power with a big majority in the legislature. Indira's handling of this situation brought her a fair share of renown.

Conditions in the state of Bombay confronted Indira with another big problem. In 1956, the former administrative units in the states of the Republic of India had been reorganized, chiefly on the basis of language. In all the states except Bombay and Punjab, which were bilingual, reorganization was on the basis of the language spoken by the majority of the people. But the Bombay State had within its boundaries Maharashtrians speaking Marathi and Gujaratis speaking Gujarati, which led to demands for the creation of a Gujarati-speaking state and a Marathi-speaking state. Riots occurred in both Gujarat and Maharashtra.

Indira went to Maharashtra to make her own survey. How did the people feel? She found out, and on returning to Delhi she reported her findings. First she met with the Maharashtra members of the Parliament and then appointed a committee of inquiry to examine the facts she had gathered. The committee recommended that the government divide Bombay State into two new states: Maharashtra, with Bombay as the capital, and Gujarat, with Ahmadabad as the capital. The Working Committee accepted this recommendation, and on May 1, 1960, the two states were formally established.

During her strenuous trip Indira had not been well, and on her arrival in Delhi she required medical treatment. Two leading doctors of Bombay were sent to Delhi to examine her. They found a kidney disorder that necessitated an operation.

As Indira's tenure of the office of President of the Congress drew to a close, the Working Committee tried to persuade her to stand for re-election. She declined. In February, 1960, Kamrj Nadar was elected President.

18

"After Nehru, Who?"

ON JAWAHAR'S SECOND OFFICIAL VISIT to the United States, in November 1961, Indira again accompanied him. He had been invited by President John F. Kennedy, for whose intellectual qualities and political skills he had great admiration. In some respects Jawaharlal Nehru and John Kennedy were alike: both were dynamic and kept things moving, they were defenders of the freedom of man, they welcomed responsibility, they had a passion for achievement, and both had that special quality called charisma. Indira and Jawahar were delighted to meet Jacqueline, the first lady, and Caroline and John, Jr. The President expressed his deep interest in Indian affairs, and Jawahar invited the Kennedys to India to see for themselves the progress made by a newly independent country, whose constitution of 1949 had been modeled after the Constitution of the United States. But Jacqueline came alone early in 1962, for the President's work prevented his leaving Washington at that time.

Jawahar asked me to be in Delhi for the occasion. "Though Indu and I have been their guests," he said, "you know them better and we feel that she will be more informal with you." Raja and I had met the Kennedys in 1956 in Washington at the home of Senator Sherman Cooper (he had been United States ambassador to India) and his charming wife Lorraine. Among the guests at a dinner party they gave for us were Senator and Mrs. Kennedy. Both these senators were trying to interest the United States in giving long-term aid to India instead of yearly allocations. Senator Kennedy and Raja had a long discussion on India's economic development and American aid.

On her visit to India, Jacqueline Kennedy and her large entourage of security officers and secretarial staff were the guests of my brother and stayed in the Prime Minister's House. Our people had heard a lot about the Kennedys, and for them John Kennedy had become a magical name. Wherever Jackie went in Delhi, huge crowds cheered her with affection. I was happy to see her again and to meet her sister, Princess Lee Radziwill. They were charming guests.

When the brief visit was over, Indira left for a lecture engagement in the United States. I had planned to return to Bombay, but the house seemed suddenly so quiet after the hum of social activities that I did not want to leave Jawahar alone. He was not well, yet he kept his heavy morning-to-midnight schedule. One day after lunch he went to his bedroom. I followed him and found him getting into bed. This was unusual. I took his temperature, sent for his doctor, and requested his secretary to cancel all engagements. Around 6 P.M. he woke up with a start and was quite angry that he had not been awakened.

His illness was obviously serious, and I was terribly worried. I kept a vigil at his bedside. Two doctors who stayed in the house were constantly on call, but after a while it became apparent to me that the medicines and diets they prescribed were doing no good, for Jawahar grew steadily weaker. I sent frantic cables to Indira to come home, but the doctors kept cabling her assurances that her father's health was improving.

I wanted to send for our old family doctor, Bidhan Roy, who was stationed in Calcutta (he held the office of chief minister of West Bengal). But on every long-distance call, the lines to Calcutta were reported as being out of order. As a last resort I turned to Lal Bahadur Shastri for help. He came to the house, listened to my complaints, and chided me affectionately for being overanxious. However, he too felt anxiety. He rang up Dr. Roy, urging him to come.

The next morning I met Dr. Roy at the airport so that we could have a talk before his consultation with the other doctors. He put his arms around me and cautioned me not to be hysterical.

"Hello, old man," he said in his booming voice as he entered Jawahar's room.

In the feeble voice of a very sick man, Jawahar replied, "Whom are you calling an old man, when you are ten years older than I? Did Betty send for you?"

After his examination of the patient, Dr. Roy went to the room assigned to the doctors in attendance, where he studied the temperature charts and prescriptions. He told them that they had erred in their diagnosis and treatment, threw out all the medicines, and prescribed a totally different regimen. He stayed for three days to watch over the patient.

The new regimen proved beneficial, and Jawahar gradually recovered. On Indira's return I left for Bombay. At Jawahar's good-bye kiss and his "Thank you, darling," I broke into tears.

Jawahar resumed his routine, but at a reduced work schedule. He seemed rather frail and had lost some of his vitality. Congress leaders began to wonder if he was well enough to carry the burdens of his office. Rumors spread about various possible successors. There was talk of a syndicate of leaders: would X, Y, and Z take over the government? British and American journalists played up cries of "After Nehru, who?" and "After Nehru, what?"

In a picturesque metaphor, an Indian journalist wrote, "Under the shade of the banyan tree nothing grows," suggesting not only a likeness between the All-India personality of Jawahar and the far-spreading banyan tree but also the absence of any other All-India person of his grand mold.

Some suggested that Jawahar should name a successor. When asked whom he would nominate, he replied that the people would make the choice, in the democratic way. Was he grooming Indira for the post? He firmly denied it. To an interviewer he said:

I am certainly not grooming her for anything of the sort. That does not mean she should not be called to occupy any position of responsibility after me. It is well known that I did not groom her or help her in any way to become the Congress President, but she did, and I am told by people who do not like me or my policies that she made a very good President. Sometimes she chose a line of her own against my way of thinking, which was the right thing to do, but what I want to point out is the fact that I did not choose her or groom her for that high post, probably the highest post in the country. The people chose her. The Congress did so. . . . In fact, for some time I was mentally opposed to the idea, but she was chosen and we worked more like normal political colleagues than a father-and-daughter combination. We agreed on some things. We differed on others. Indira has a strong independent mind of her own, as she should have.

Another time he said, "I would not like to appear to encourage some sort of dynastic arrangement. That would be wholly undemocratic and an undesirable thing."

To everyone's surprise, Jawahar brought Lal Bahadur Shastri into the Cabinet as Minister Without Portfolio. Lal Bahadurji was only about five feet tall—not an imposing figure. Many thought that he lacked the qualities that would enable him to rise to the prime ministership. But Jawahar knew the abilities of this quiet men.

Ever since China's invasion of Tibet in 1959, China had been infiltrating northwest India at far-flung points, and there had been minor skirmishes between Chinese and Indian troops. Nevertheless, Jawahar continued to trust the Chinese avowals of friendship. In October, 1962, when Raja and I were on vacation in Simla, our plans to go up into the hills to the Tibetan border were suddenly canceled by the commander of the Western Forces, General Daulat Singh, an old friend of ours. He asked us to come to his house and told us that the Chinese had invaded Ladakh and that the roads were chock full of military convoys. We hastened to Delhi to be with Jawahar.

In October and November, a force of twenty thousand Chinese troops broke through the Se-La Pass—a wild Himalayan gorge that had always been considered impregnable. The Indian army, under the command of General Kaul, was routed. General Kaul disappeared from Tezpur, the headquarters of the command, and the whole of the Northeast Frontier Agency (NEFA) lay open for the invader. The Chinese occupied some fourteen thousand square miles of Indian territory.

For India, the military reverses were a calamity, and the heaviest blow fell on Jawahar in his disillusionment over China's perfidy. He felt that he, in trusting China, had misled the Indian people. In his speech before the Parliament, he did not spare himself, but he realized that he had to rouse the country to action. The Defense Minister, Krishna Menon, who had been responsible for putting General Kaul in command, was replaced by Y. B. Chavan, who instituted changes to make for a stronger, more modern Indian army. Jawahar obtained support and military aid from the United States and the Commonwealth countries.

A Citizens' Defense Committee, headed by Indira, and local defense committees were formed to mobilize the support of all Indians. Indira went to troubled areas—to Tezpur, where the withdrawal of the Indian army caused panic, and to riot-torn Jahalpur—to restore the people's confidence in their government. And she collected and dispatched warm clothing, food, drugs, and other necessities to the Jawans (the Indian troops) in the high altitudes of NEFA and Ladakh.

For reasons known only to themselves, the Chinese suddenly announced a unilateral cease-fire and withdrew their forces. Political and military experts conjectured that the Chinese had hoped for large-scale chaos in India resulting in a takeover by the Communist party of India and that they decided against extending their lines of communication when the chaos did not materialize. For India, it was an uneasy peace.

With the shattering of his faith in Asian solidarity and the growing internal problems of the country, Jawahar's health declined. His old vigor and zest for life had gone. He felt the burden of his age.

19

"Love and Affection from the Indian People"

CRITICISM OF HIS ECONOMIC planning policies for India actuated Jawahar's determination to defend his program before the Congress. He prepared a speech for delivery at the 1964 session, which was held at Bhuvaneshwar in Orissa early in January. He made an effective appeal. Just as he was bringing his speech to completion, he suffered a stroke.

Radio broadcasts brought the news to Bombay. I wanted to go to Orissa at once, but Indira phoned that she was taking him back to Delhi and that I should go there.

By the end of the month, Jawahar showed definite gains. With his great reserves of natural vigor and courage, he slowly got well. However, he tired easily, and his left foot dragged a little as he walked. By April he was making speeches again. He and Indira came to Bombay for the May meeting of the Congress party. On May 18, after the meeting, I rode with them to the airport, where large crowds had collected to bid him good-bye. As the plane was readying for the takeoff, I ran up the ramp to give my brother a farewell hug. That was the last time I saw him.

On the morning of May 27, Nan and I were summoned to Delhi. I phoned Indira. In a faint, anguished voice, she said: "Papu is collapsing. Come soon." A government plane was sent for us. On our flight, news came that he was no more.

Outside the closed wrought-iron gates of Teen Murti House, a mighty crowd was surging forward, in tumult over the death of their idol. The house was filled with Cabinet ministers, members of Parliment and the Congress party, diplomats, and relatives. As we entered the room where Jawahar lay, we found Indira sitting motionless on the floor—near her father. That night, when his body was brought downstairs to lie in state, she stood by his side as if turned to stone, unconscious of the thousands who walked past to pay their last homage. Though braver than the rest of us, she broke down the next morning, when day brought the full realization of her loss. I followed Indira to her suite, and there, in the privacy of her room, she sobbed her heart out. But she quickly gained control of herself and asked me to attend to the wants of those who had come from afar—to see that they got breakfast. Then she washed her face and went again to stand by her father's side.

For guidance on funeral arrangements, Indira turned to Lal Bahadur Shastri. Jawahar, in his last will and testament, had expressed his desire for cremation:

> When I die, I should like my body to be cremated. . . . A small handful of these ashes should be thrown into the Ganga. . . .

The major portion of my ashes should, however, be disposed of otherwise. I want these to be carried high up into the air in an aeroplane and scattered from that height over the fields where the peasants of India toil, so that they might mingle with the dust and soil of India and become an indistinguishable part of India.[1]

The funeral cortege proceeded from Teen Murti House to Shanti Vana (Abode of Peace; the cremation grounds). The gun carriage bearing Jawahar's body was drawn by men chosen from the armed forces. It moved slowly through lines of soldiers, police, and masses of mourners. People wept, showered flowers on the gun carriage, and acclaimed Jawahar. They called out to Indira, who rode in an open car with her son Sanjay (the older son, Rajiv, was to arrive the following day from Cambridge). In their sympathy for Indira, the people wanted to share her grief. The funeral rite ended with the filing of family, officials, diplomats, and close friends past the pyre, more scattering of flowers, and the lighting of the pyre. The ashes were placed in a large bronze urn and several small urns.

On the thirteenth day following the rites, the ashes in the large urn were taken by special train to Allahabad for immersion in the Ganges. The five-hundred-mile journey through the plains of India's heartland took twenty-four hours, for the train had to slow down all along the route. Millions lined up everywhere, in the villages and the open countryside, to get a glimpse of the urn that contained the ashes of their leader. The urn was in an open, gracefully decorated car. Indira, with hands folded, sat on the floor. The crowds felt a kinship with her, in their common loss.

Love for Jawahar was strikingly evident throughout the long journey. In his lifetime, he had himself always cherished the love of his people, as manifested in the opening words of his testament and will: "I have received so much love and affection from the Indian people that nothing that I can do can repay even a small fraction of it, and indeed there can be no repayment of so precious a thing as affection."[2]

In Allahabad, the people paid an impressive but more silent homage to the great man who had lived among them. Again crowds lined the road as we proceeded to the Ganges. Indira, her sons, Nan, and I entered a boat to take the urn far out in the river. Rajiv and Sanjay poured the ashes into the Ganges.

On our return to Delhi, Indira took one of the small urns on a flight to Kashmir, to scatter Jawahar's ashes over mountains and streams. Nan and I took urns on flights in the environs of Delhi to scatter his ashes over fields. And Cabinet ministers scattered his ashes over the soil of other parts of India.

On the day of Jawahar's death, an emergency committee of the Cabinet appointed Gulzaril Nanda, the Home Minister, as acting Prime Minister. During the next days the Congress Working Committee held meetings. It authorized the president of the Congress party, Kumaraswami Kamaraj, to make a recommendation on the choice for a Nehru successor. He asserted his preference: Lal Bahadur Shastri.

The Parliament had a choice between Morarji Desai, who had announced his candidacy; Nanda, the acting Prime Minister; Lal Bahadur Shastri, who, as Minister

Without Portfolio, had worked closely with Jawahar. Indira, in her grief, was unwilling to take on the burden of office. On June 2, Shastri was unanimously elected leader of the Congress party and invited to form a government. A week later he was sworn in as Prime Minister.

Shastri asked Indira to take over the Foreign Ministry. She declined the offer, for she wished to devote herself to the establishment of a memorial to her father. But Shastri was not to be put off. He offered her other ministerial posts. The daughter of Nehru, he said, would lend prestige to his Cabinet and make it easier for him to carry on, especially because of her familiarity with both internal and external affairs of government. At last she yielded, by accepting a lesser post—Minister of Information and Broadcasting.

20

A Cabinet Minister

As a minister, Indira was allotted a government-owned house. She moved to 1 Safdar Jung Road, a much smaller house than Teen Murti. It had only four bedrooms, two of which had to be converted for reception and office use. The surrounding grounds were small—really too small for the crowds that came early every morning. These daily visits of the people were a surviving custom of the days when crowds came to Jawahar for his *darshan*—merely to look at a dearly loved and respected person. By means of this ritual, Indira met the people, listened to their grievances, and often lessened their hardships. Like Jawahar, she drew inspiration and strength from talking with the people, who in turn gave her their affection and loyalty.

The constitution of India requires a minister to be a member of one of the two houses of Parliament. Members of the lower house are elected, but Indira, after the recent loss of her father, was not ready to cope with the rigors of campaigning. She therefore chose a seat in the Rajya Sabha, the upper house, to which she was nominated. And so began her apprenticeship in parliamentary practices and in the functions of the Ministry of Information and Broadcasting.

In a country like India, with its vast illiteracy and lack of communication, radio and television can have an important role in bringing education into the home. But Indian programs had not even begun to achieve the quality or daily number of hours of broadcasting time commonly encountered in more affluent countries. Broadcasts reached a very small number of listeners, for receiving sets were beyond the average man's purse.

Indira thought up a way of getting programs into more homes. She encouraged "the manufacture of inexpensive transistor radios with short-wave reception that would pick up more than one station. Only the most expensive Indian-made radios had a range of more than a few hundred miles." And "she opened the air waves, which up to then had been a government monopoly and the mouth-piece of the ruling party, to members of the opposition parties and to independent commentators."[1]

New Delhi had a small television station; its programs had little merit. Indira injected popular interest when she scheduled a program of social significance—a family-planning program on birth control, with explanations of artificial methods of contraception. It reflected her concern over India's soaring birth rate.

Her ministry also had administrative functions in regard to the cinema, the theater, and the art of the dance.

Indira promoted modern techniques in these fields, organized an international films festival, and gave governmental aid to theater and dance groups. She gave the Board of Film Censors a new look by appointing to it men and women of progressive (not ultramoralist) outlook.

Because Indira had met the leaders of nations in her many visits abroad and had been present at important diplomatic negotiations, she held a high place in the Cabinet hierarchy. Her first foreign stop as a representative of the government of India was made when the Soviet Union invited her to Moscow. Nikita Khrushchev had been replaced by Aleksei Kosygin and Leonid Brezhnev. Would the Russian policy toward India change? Indira came back to Delhi with assurances from the new Soviet leaders that they valued Indo-Soviet friendship and that economic and military aid to India would continue. The visit proved her adeptness in diplomacy.

Her next engagement took her to New York, where she presided at the inauguration of the Nehru Memorial Exhibition. The show, which was formally opened by Vice-President Hubert Humphrey, depicted Jawahar's life and work in an assemblage of photographs arranged chronologically, with historical and biographical notes.

Jacqueline Kennedy attended the opening. It was her first public appearance after the assassination of her husband, and was evidence of her friendly feelings toward India. Her graciousness was apparent in a little incident when she extended her hand to greet the guard on duty at the steps leading to the platform. He was a guard of the President of India's staff. Tall and handsome, he looked a wonderful figure of a man in his uniform and blue turban as he stood at attention. When Mrs. Kennedy, having recognized him as the guard who had been posted at her door on her visit to India, wanted to shake hands with him, he looked straight ahead and stood like a rock. Realizing that he was on duty, she smilingly withdrew. Later he bowed to Mrs. Kennedy and apologized for his seeming discourtesy.

Social welfare work continued to take much of Indira's time. She was frank to admit shortcomings in social action. "The governmental program," she wrote in an article, "is certainly expanding, although not always so systematically as one would wish. Often enough it is put in the charge of people who have no special sympathy or knowledge. A number of laws have been passed, but can we honestly say that they are being implemented?"

For months Pakistan had been sending infiltrators into Kashmir, with instructions to blow up bridges and dislocate communications upon a prearranged signal. Pakistan hoped that the Kashmiris would rise in revolt and join the invaders. Instead, the government of Kashmir killed or captured thousands of these infiltrators and the population remained loyal to India.

In September, 1965, the Pakistani army invaded India. Pakistan mounted an attack on the Jammu District, so as to cut off the road link of the Kashmir Valley with India. She attacked with tanks and modern weapons and sent her powerful air force to open the road through the Punjab plains to New Delhi. Radio Pakistan announced that New Delhi would be in their hands in three days but they never came anywhere near Delhi. The Indian army bravely defended our territory and then took the offensive, crossing the Pakistani border and advancing toward

Lahore, where both sides incurred heavy losses in fierce fighting.

The Pakistanis had the very latest military equipment. It had been supplied by the United States for use in defense against Russia and China—as a consequence of Pakistan's having joined the Central Treaty Organization (CENTO) and the Southeast Asia Treaty Organization (SEATO). President Eisenhower had given assurances to India that American armament sent to Pakistan would not be used against India. When India reminded the United States of this assurance, all that the United States did was to cut off military aid to both Pakistan and India. (India had been receiving limited military aid since the Chinese attack of 1962.)

Poorly equipped as our air force was, with much slower planes, our men handled their planes effectively and drove Pakistan's superior American planes from the skies in many a dogfight. Pakistan had made the mistake of believing that the Indian soldier, ignominiously routed by the Chinese at the Se-La Pass in 1962, was a cardboard soldier. That defeat the Indian army had taken to heart, and the army had been modernized. It was now ably led by General J. N. Chaudhuri.

Indira was the first Cabinet member to go to the battle-front. She visited troops in the field and the wounded in frontline hospitals. To the Jawans (GI's) she spoke proudly of their devotion and achievements. She gave them a sense of their own personal participation in the defense of a country well worth fighting for.

In trips to various cities, she revitalized the local citizens' defense committees to make supreme efforts for defensive plans. The people rallied to the support of their brave Jawans who were laying down their lives in defense of India. Yet no one wanted the war. We were aware of the economic consequences of war to a poor and starving population. We could have taken Lahore in West Pakistan, but we had no designs to acquire territory from Pakistan.

Indian victories made Pakistan anxious for peace. All her calculations in Kashmir had gone wrong, and China had not come to her aid by opening another front in the east. The big powers strongly urged a cessation of hostilities, and mediation proposals came from various countries. When Premier Aleksei Kosygin of the Soviet Union asked Lal Bahadur Shastri and President Ayub Khan of Pakistan to meet with him at Tashkent for a discussion of a possible settlement, both accepted his invitation.

The meeting, held in early January, 1966, ended in an agreement that both armies would withdraw behind their respective borders and the establishment of a cease-fire line, which India and Pakistan agreed to respect. More important was the agreement of both nations to renounce force as an instrument to settle disputes between them. This virtually amounted to a no-war pact which India had been repeatedly offering to Pakistan. Other points included in the Tashkent Pact were noninterference with each other's internal affairs; halting hostile propaganda; resumption of economic, communication, and cultural ties; and implementation of already existing agreements.

To celebrate the signing of the Tashkent Pact, the Russians gave a banquet. On returning to the villa assigned to him, Shastri telephoned his son to inquire how India had reacted to the pact. He was worried particularly about the agreement to withdraw our forces from strategic passes that belonged to Kashmir. During the night Shastri had a heart attack and died.

India was profoundly shocked. The country mourned the loss of the second Prime Minister in their history, who had been in office only eighteen months. Lal Bahadur Shastri had won the respect and love of our people.

21

Shastri's Brief Administration and the Election of Indira Gandhi

THE PERSONAL PRESTIGE and popularity of Lal Bahadur Shastri soared during his administration, which lasted only from June 9, 1964, to January 11, 1966. As a true Gandhian, he had devoted followers among the people. They admired him for his performance in the war with Pakistan and at the Tashkent Conference. He encouraged Cabinet deliberations, sought a consensus in decision-making, and relied on well-chosen policy advisers. In the tense dispute with Pakistan over the Rann of Kutch—a large salt marsh in Gujarat State—he promoted a peaceful settlement. He was a man of peace who led the country firmly but gently.

But Shastri's term of office was also marked by adversities. The war expenditures and the failure of the monsoon winds to bring an adequate rainfall had a disastrous effect on the national economy. People prayed for rain that did not come. The summer of 1965 was marked by drought, resulting in the threat of famine and in food riots. The third five-year plan, which had been formulated under Jawahar, failed to achieve the goals in agricultural and industrial output. The nation was in need of capital resources to push industrial and agricultural production forward. The economy was stagnant.

In addition, crises developed both at the Cabinet level and in state legislatures. There were language riots. The constitution of India had provided for the introduction of Hindi as the official language by 1965. India has fourteen basic languages, embracing eight hundred dialects, and in the south resentment arose against the constitutional provision. The Tamil-speaking people of Madras were particularly incensed. They burned down trains and public buildings. Police fired into the mobs and killed at least sixty people. The Parliament, which is predominantly Hindi-speaking, was hostile and averse to Shastri's moderation in settling for compromises. The language riots spread in Uttar Pradesh and Madhya Pradesh in the north.

The worst drought that summer and the worst food riots occurred in Uttar Pradesh State, Shastri's own home ground. The problem of how to feed the people, in a situation of a growing deficit in the nation's balance of international payments, caused conflicts among members of Parliament. Agricultural production was low. Fertilizer projects remained unfulfilled. Meantime the population was increasing at the rate of twelve million a year.

The United States sent aid in the form of large shipments of grain, and Indo-American relations were good. However, when Shastri criticized the United States for its bombing of North Vietnam, relations deteriorated. President Johnson canceled a planned invitation to Shastri to visit Washington. (President Johnson did plan to invite him early in January, 1966—a plan that had to remain unrealized because of the sad event of January 11 in Tashkent.)

In the early morning of January 11, as soon as the news of Shastri's death reached New Delhi, the post of acting Prime Minister was given to Gulzarilal Nanda as the member of the Cabinet with the highest seniority.

Under the constitution, the majority party in the Parliament—that is, the Congress party—elects its leader, and the leader is called upon to form the government. The elected leader selects the members of his Cabinet. But the suddenness of the need for electing a new Prime Minister catapulted the Congress into controversy. Leaders of the Congress Working Committee were divided while the state governments pulled in different directions, asserting their personal independence.

New parties found their opportunity to discredit the Congress party. The Swatantra (Freedom) party, a conservative group, leaned toward the West. The Jan Sangh party (a people's party) was a militant group of rightists.

Now there were many who claimed leadership, chief among them were Morarji Desai, the former Finance Minister, a man of ardent zeal and many puritanical fads and Y. B. Chavan, the Defense Minister, who had successfully rejuvenated the army in the Indo-Pakistani war. Morarji and Chavan had once worked concurrently in the state cabinet of Bombay, before the state was divided into Maharashtra and Gujarat. When Morarji joined the central government, he passed on his chief ministership of the Bombay State to his trusted colleague, Chavan, expecting him to keep the Marathi-speaking and Gujarati-speaking groups from separating into two separate states. But Chavan set about to promote the partition of the state with the prize city of Bombay as the capital of Maharashtra. Morarji considered this a breach of faith, and the two men became political enemies.

Among others who claimed leadership were Gulzarilal Nanda, Jagjivan Ram, and S. K. Patil, the Congress party boss of Bombay and a leading light of the "Syndicate" of political bosses of West Bengal, Bombay, and Madras.

The Syndicate controlled the Congress party in nine states. Kamaraj, the Congress president, had been somewhat estranged from the Syndicate because he had insisted on continuing as President for a second term. The members of the Syndicate functioned as kingmakers. In order to maintain their power, they preferred a weak and pliable person as head of state. They knew they could not boss Morarji Desai and therefore opposed him. Their choice was Nanda, but he had no backing within the party.

The Congress Working Committee was concerned about the future of the party, for the economic crisis and stories of corruption among some Congress ministers had brought on a general dissatisfaction of the people. Only an effective and popular election campaigner—one who had the charisma of Jawahar—could hurdle the obstacles to unity.

It was suggested to Kamaraj that he should himself be a contender for the post, but he disbarred his own candidacy. He is a self-taught man of the people and speaks only Tamil, his mother tongue. A prime minister of a country as multilingual as India, where the majority speak or understand Hindi, would have difficulty addressing an audience. He picked Indira as his choice. He thought that she alone could rally the people to a strong government and maintain the unity of the party. She was widely known nationally and internationally, had no enemies, and had become an All-India figure.

Kamaraj suggested her name to the Working Committee, and made the further suggestion that it would be best if the nominee were selected by consensus and unanimously elected. Morarji, however, insisted that there should be an open election by the party without any interference by the Congress Working Committee. In hectic canvassing, he claimed that he had better qualifications for leadership than Indira. In answer to this claim, she commented, "It is for the members of the Parliament to decide whom they want as the Prime Minister."

While the candidates were hard at work building up a following among Congress members, Kamaraj assumed his role of kingmaker. Putting all his strength behind the election of Indira, he called upon the chief ministers of the ten states that were administered by the Congress party to ask them to see that members of Parliament from their states would vote for his nominee. He asked Indira to stand for election as the leader of the Congress party in Parliament. She would, of course, have preferred a unanimous choice, but the challenge inherent in an election did not bother her. Nor was she deterred by a note from Kamaraj hinting that she was only an interim candidate. "We are old," he wrote, "and the next time you wish to run we may not be around." She knew that the people were behind her, whatever the party bosses might do.

When reporters asked about her willingness to face a contest, she said, "I will do what Mr. Kamaraj wants me to do." In other words, she would be prepared if the majority of the Congress Working Committee drafted her.

The date of the election was fixed for January 19, 1966, when the Congress party members of Parliament were to elect the leader.

I was beside myself with excitement. Indira seemed to me to be alone. Her sons were in England. And I wanted to be with her. Though my doctors had instructed me to remain in bed because of a fracture of the spine due to a fall, I left Bombay by plane for New Delhi.

In the early morning of January 19, while the town, still asleep, lay shrouded in mist, Indira made two pilgrimages. First she went to Rajghat, the memorial to Gandhiji on the bank of the Jumna River. Standing before the *Samadhi* (the platform where his body was laid for cremation), she offered a prayer for his blessing. Then she went to Shanti Vana, the place of Jawahar's cremation, as if she meant to keep her tryst with the two who had fashioned her life and molded her destiny. As she stood before her father's *Samadhi*, she thought of a letter he had written her on her thirteenth birthday:

> Be brave, and all the rest follows. If you are brave, you will not fear and will not do anything of which you are ashamed. . . . Let us make friends with the sun and work in the light and do nothing secretly and furtively. . . . And if you do so, my dear, you will grow up a child of the light, unafraid and serene and unruffled, whatever may happen.

Indira also paid a visit to Teen Murti House. She went to her father's room (it has been kept intact as it was during his lifetime), where she recalled the Robert Frost poem that he had scribbled on a pad lying on his bedside table:

> *The woods are lovely, dark and deep,*
> *But I have promises to keep,*
> *And miles to go before I sleep.*

Now that it was her turn to keep the promises, she may have had some doubts about the difficult task that lay ahead. She may have remembered another Robert Frost poem:

> *The king said to his son: "Enough of this!*
> *The Kingdom is yours to finish as you please,*
> *I'm getting out tonight. Here, take the crown."*
>
> *But the prince drew away his hand in time*
> *To avoid what he wasn't sure he wanted.*

Indira's car was waiting for me at the airport to take me to Parliament House. I pushed my way through the large crowds to the Central Hall, where the voting was taking place. I remained outside, leaning against a marble pillar to rest my painful back. Indira saw me and came to embrace me. She said, "Puphi [meaning "father's sister"], I told you not to come. With your injured back you should be resting." She got me a chair and rushed back into the Central Hall.

After a while a man came out and asked the reporters and photographers to go into the hall, and he escorted me to a chair inside.

At about 3 P.M. the presiding officer handed Kamaraj the totals of the vote. The meeting, which had been noisy with people chatting and moving about, suddenly came to a pin-drop silence. Kamaraj, his smile showing that the outcome was all that he wished, announced the result in Tamil, which only a few people understood. Then it was translated into English: Indira had 355 votes against Morarji Desai's 169. Indira had been elected the leader of the Congress party in the Parliament and as such would form the government.

A burst of applause and cheering drowned the voice of Kamaraj as he tried to call the meeting to order so that Indira might come to the platform to join him and Nanda. Indira was modestly sitting way back among the members of the Parliament. Morarji, sitting near the front, looked stern and grim.

As Indira made her way to the dais, members jumped up from their seats and clustered around her to shake her hand in congratulation. Television cameras focused their bright lights on her. She was dressed in a plain white *khadi* sari. On the brownish-gray Kashmiri shawl draped around her shoulders was a corsage of one red rose, the Jawahar symbol. As she passed Morarji, she bowed to him with folded hands in the Indian fashion and said, "Will you bless me in the tasks that I have ahead, Morarjibhai?"

Unsmilingly, he replied, "I give you my blessing."

Indira, now on the dais, began her address in these words: "As I stand before you my thoughts go back to our great leaders: Mahatma Gandhi, at whose feet I grew up; Panditji, my father; and Lal Bahadur Shastri. These leaders have shown the way and I want to go along the same path."

The crowd of more than ten thousand gathered outside Parliament House had given her a hearty reception on her arrival for the meeting. Seeing the red rose, they had greeted her with excited cries of *"Lal Gulab Zindabad"* ("Long live the red rose"). Now, as people streamed out of the Central Hall, someone shouted, "Is it a boy? A girl?"

"A girl" came the answer, and the crowd surged forward, joyously cheering Indira: *"Jawaharlal Nehru ki jai!"* ("Hail Jawaharlal Nehru!")

I could not get near Indira in the milling crowd, so I joined Nan in her car and we drove to her home. After hurriedly gulping down a cup of tea and an omelette, I left for Indira's house. I embraced her and then we went out on the lawn where the press awaited her.

About seven months before her election as Prime Minister, Indira had written an article for a New Delhi newspaper in which she expressed her faith in her father's policies. At the time she had no thought of herself as head of state. She had a theme in mind for all Indians: their responsibility to make a mature nation. But her words became, in a sense, a prophecy of her own objectives as the official head of the country. It was in 1965, during Shastri's administration, that she made this plea to the people of India:

A year ago he [Jawahar] left us, but his spirit is still with us and will so remain to inspire us, to strengthen our faltering steps and to give us faith in ourselves and our people. Let us, then, endeavor to be worthy of his memory. Let us dedicate ourselves to the monumental task of giving substance to his dream of making India a progressive and mature nation.

On January 25, 1966, Indira Gandhi took the oath of office as Prime Minister of India.

22

Political Power
Entrusted to a Woman

THE WORLD'S LARGEST DEMOCRACY had chosen a woman as head of state. No major country had ever before elected a woman to the most important office of the nation. In a small Asian country—namely, Ceylon—Sirimavo Bandaranaike, the widow of the assassinated Premier, had been elected Premier in 1960, but her succession to her husband's position was merely symbolic of Ceylon's affection and regard for the assassinated Premier. Mrs. Bandaranaike had had no political experience. But India's election of Indira Gandhi as Prime Minister was a historical first. She was chosen because of her progressive, modern outlook, her dedicated service, and her valuable experience in politics and government.

The reaction of the world was one of surprise that a woman should wield political power over a nation of half a billion people. The astonishment was greatest in the

United States, where the election of a woman President is still unimaginable.

At the invitation of President Johnson, Indira began a state visit to Washington on March 27, 1966. The fact that the visiting head of state was a woman fascinated the American press. Some rather rudely talked of petticoat rule in government office; some hinted that she was merely a decorative mascot or a convenient façade for a party clique. Reporters besieged her with questions. Could she handle a man-size job? Was she a feminist? Did she believe that a way had been opened for women to have a greater role in politics? She replied: "I do not regard myself as a woman. I am a person with a job to do."

My assumption of office as Prime Minister has occasioned no surprise in India, where women have for years played a prominent role in the freedom struggle, in politics, and in public life. We have women engineers, women governors, women ambassadors, women judges, and women diplomats and administrators. Many of our village councils have women members, and some of them consist entirely of women. Women have a tremendously important role to play in every field of human endeavor. My position does not add to or detract from this fundamental truth.

To the women of India, who have never been feminists, the militant suffragettes of Western countries appeared to be man-haters. The question of equality with men, or superiority over them, does not arise for them. Indian religion, culture, and tradition point to the concept that man and woman complement each other.

In Indian mythology, Ardhanareshwar (a deity half man, half woman) symbolizes the essential oneness of man and woman. The Hindu pantheon comprises gods who are always referred to by joint names of spouses (for example, Radha Krishna, Sita Rama), and there are female divinities such as Shakti, the goddess of strength, Lakshmi, the goddess of wealth and prosperity, and Saraswati, the goddess of knowledge and culture.

In the caves of Ajanta, the fresco paintings covering the walls (they date back to the third to the fifth centuries) show the reverence of men for women. In describing these remarkable frescoes, an art critic wrote: "I can think of no parallel to this frank and chivalrous woman worship as depicted in Ajanta. Nowhere else has woman received such perfect understanding and homage."

In the ancient culture of India, there was almost no seclusion of women, but their legal status had its drawbacks, as it did in Western society: "Bad as the legal position of women was in ancient India, judged by modern standards, it was far better than in ancient Greece, Rome, early Christianity, the Canon Law of medieval Europe, and indeed till right up to comparatively modern times at the beginning of the nineteenth century."[1]

In the medieval period, the Afghan conquest of India had the effect of synthesizing old ways and new. Jawahar, writing his manuscript of *The Discovery of India* while in Ahmadnagar Fort prison, had this to say about changes in the Indian social structure, especially as they applied to the position of women:

Among the unfortunate developments that took place in India was the growth of purdah or the seclusion of women. . . . In India there had been previously some segregation of the sexes among the aris-

tocracy, as in many other countries and notably in
ancient Greece. . . . Purdah seems to have grown in
India during Moghul times, when it became a mark
of status and prestige among both Hindus and Moslems. This custom of seclusion of women spread
especially among the upper classes of those areas
where Moslem influence had been most marked—in
the great central and eastern block comprising Delhi,
the United Provinces, Rajputana, Bihar, and Bengal.

I have no doubt at all that among the causes of
India's decay in recent centuries, purdah or the seclusion of women holds an important place. I am
even more convinced that the complete ending of
this barbarous custom is essential before India can
have a progressive social life. That it injures woman
is obvious enough, but the injury to man, to the
growing child who has to spend much of its time
among women in purdah, and to social life generally
is equally great. Fortunately this evil practice is fast
disappearing among the Hindus, more slowly among
the Moslems. The strongest factor in this liquidation
of purdah has been the Congress political and social
movements which have drawn tens of thousands of
middle-class women into some kind of public activity. Gandhiji has been, and is, a fierce opponent of
purdah and has called it a "vicious and brutal
custom" which has kept woman backward and un-
developed. . . . Gandhi urged that women should
have the same liberty and opportunity for self-devel-
opment as man. "Good sense must govern the relations between the two sexes. There should be no barrier erected between them. Their mutual behaviour
should be natural and spontaneous." Gandhi has indeed written and spoken with passion in favor of

women's equality and freedom, and has bitterly condemned their domestic slavery.[2]

Another feature of the old Indian social structure bur-
densome to women was the joint family system, in which
the individual was subordinated. Each family member
shared in the common property. But if a daughter married, she belonged to her new family and therefore had no
share in the property of the family she was born into, in
accordance with the Hindu law of inheritance, and became dependent on her husband or son.

The custom of child marriages (brought on by Muslim
invaders who carried away the nubile girls) also imposed
a burden on women. Such a marriage was never consummated until the girl attained puberty. If the boy happened
to die before the marriage was consummated, the girl was
sentenced to a life of restricted widowhood. Chastity became the supreme virtue, and sex the greatest sin, which
was contrary to the concept of life as depicted in Hindu
sculptures and temple frescoes.

Despite the *purdah* and child marriages, women continued to be respected and honored in many ways, and
they had a fair measure of freedom, taking part in social,
cultural, and religious activities. Thousands of women responded to Gandhi's appeal for their participation in the
nation's fight for independence. In a resolution of 1931,
the Congress Working Committee recognized the services
rendered by women:

> And we record our homage and deep admiration
> for the womanhood of India who, in the hour of peril
> for the motherland, forsook the shelter of their
> homes and, with unfailing courage and endurance,

stood shoulder to shoulder with their menfolk in the front line of India's national army, to share with them the sacrifices and triumphs of the struggle.

The roster of names of famous women in India's history includes thinkers and philosophers, rulers, and warriors: Razia Sultana ruled the Empire of Delhi with tact and acumen; Queen Noorjehan ruled the Mogul Empire; Rani of Jhansi led her army against the British in the 1857 war of independence and was defeated only by treachery. James Mills, the British historian notes in his *History of India* that some of the best-administered states of India were ruled by women.

Independence removed an alien rule that had impeded progress and allowed the society to stagnate. The Indian constitution gives equal rights to men and women, and with universal adult franchise, women of India came forward to take their rightful place, which they had earned by their sacrifices in the national struggle. The old and outworn Hindu law was changed, and women were given the right of inheritance. The constitution further guarantees that no citizen shall be discriminated against on grounds of sex.

Recent history has produced a galaxy of outstanding women. A poet, Sarojini Naidu, became the President of the Congress in 1925; after independence, she was governor of Uttar Pradesh. My sister Vijaya Lakshmi Pandit (Nan) was the first woman ambassador in the world, as the Indian ambassador to Moscow and to Washington, and the high commissioner to the United Kingdom; and in 1953 she was elected President of the United Nations General Assembly. Rajkumari Amrit Kaur was Minister of

Health in the government of India; she was succeeded by another woman, Dr. Sushila Nayar.

In 1966 there were fifty-nine women members of the Parliament (as against twelve in the United States Congress), and there were many women representatives in the seventeen state legislatures. Sucheta Kripalani was the chief minister of one of the largest states in India.

It should occasion no surprise that a woman was elected to be Prime Minister of India. Indira's intimate association with politics since childhood had made her a public figure, and her country chose to entrust its problems to her.

At the end of her second year in office as Prime Minister, Indira was asked whether being a woman was a handicap or an asset in politics. She answered:

I don't think my being a woman makes any difference at all. It is a question again of putting people in compartments. If you say that this job is only for a man, that man has certain qualities and capabilities that a woman does not have—then what are these qualities? Physical strength? No, if you are looking for weak points, you can find them in anybody, and I don't think a person who is head of state should think in terms of himself or herself as belonging to any group—whether it is sex, religion, or caste. If the people accept you as leader of the nation, that is all that matters.[3]

23

A Washington Dinner Party and Troubles at Home

THE PEOPLE of the United States were captivated by Indira's beauty. The orange-color sari she wore on landing in Washington was admired, and on each public occasion reporters described her clothes in detail. For days she was front-page news. Her radio broadcasts and television interviews were received with accolades.

On a bright but cold and windy March morning, President and Mrs. Johnson had greeted Indira on the White House lawn, where she arrived by helicopter after an overnight stay at colonial Williamsburg in Virginia. Mrs. Johnson presented her with a bouquet of American Beauty roses. The band played the "Morning Song of India" and the "Star-Spangled Banner."

As is customary with distinguished guests, Indira was escorted by President Johnson and a general of the army for an inspection of the guard of honor. Beside her two very tall escorts, she looked very small and delicate. The President made a speech to welcome her to the United States, and she replied with eloquence.

Formal affairs followed. The last social event was a dinner given by our cousin B. K. Nehru (we call him Bijju) and his wife Fori. He was then the Indian ambassador to the United States. Vice-President and Mrs. Humphrey were the guests of honor.

The totally unexpected visit of President Johnson just before the dinner turned everything topsy-turvy. It was his custom not to accept a return engagement from visiting heads of state, but he was so impressed with Indira that he wanted to have one more chat with her.

I was an early arrival at the house and found it full of Secret Service men. Bijju and Fori presented me to the President. Indira, wearing a coral pink sari, was sitting beside him. Their talk continued way past the dinner hour, to the consternation of the hosts, who were concerned about guests not being able to drive up to the door, for the Presidential limousines were blocking the driveway. Finally Fori invited the President to stay to dinner. At first he remonstrated, saying that his business suit was inappropriate for the occasion, and then he assented. He told his daughter Luci to go home and take Indira's two sons with her. Luci Johnson had her own engagements for the evening, so she dropped the young men at Blair House. Meanwhile Fori had her hands full changing the place cards at the table.

After the President had ordered the driveway to be cleared of Secret Service cars, the guests arrived—jeweled ladies in glamorous Parisian gowns and men in black ties. They were taken aback to see the President in a business suit. At the dinner table he monopolized Indira's attention. In a toast to honor her he made a delightful speech. "I am the man," he said, "who came to talk and stayed for dinner." Indira made a charming response.

The next day the President's plane took Indira and me to New York, where she made an *extempore* speech at a dinner for eight hundred guests given by the Economic Club of New York. Her engaging personality and her gift for making a clear presentation of what India stands for elicited many rounds of applause.

Indo-American relations were greatly improved through Indira's conversations with President Johnson. She gave an account of the suffering of the people from poverty, the bad crop years, and the priority given to agriculture in her country's efforts to raise agricultural output. She asked for an increase in aid to cope with the problem of food shortage. The President promised an additional $500 million for 1966. (In the two years from September 1964 to September 1966, the United States shipments amounted to over $1.1 billion worth of food.)

Among published reports on Indira's visit was one by William White, a columnist of the *Washington Post* who had not been particularly friendly to India. He wrote:

> No previous conference of heads of state in the time of the Johnson administration has accomplished so much for so many as has the President's parley here with Mrs. Indira Gandhi. . . . It turned out, in short, that she has been and intends to remain a moderate-minded, undoctrinaire leader of India— not in our pocket, of course, but also not at our throats.

Time Magazine made this comment:

The result of Mrs. Gandhi's visit was primarily a new mood of increased warmth and understanding between the United States and India. She and the President decided during the week that they were going roughly in the same direction, and that they could accomplish things without making demands on each other. Mrs. Gandhi proved to be not only "a very proud, very gracious, and very able lady," as the President called her, but a fiercely independent ruler with a determination equal to his own.

From Washington Indira flew to London and Paris and then to Moscow for talks with Kosygin and Brezhnev. On her return to India she was confronted with troubles. The food problem was uppermost. Vast areas in Uttar Pradesh and Bihar were faced with famine and starvation. The 1965 crops of the nation were short by fifteen million tons of food grains. Hoarding of grain and poor distribution added to the problems. Food riots occurred in the southern state of Kerala, while states like Andhra had surplus rice that they refused to share with food-shortage states.

Indira set herself to the task of revitalizing the agricultural industry. She authorized studies to be made on intensive cultivation and wide use of fertilizers and on methods of improving marketing facilities. Agricultural experts of India were asked to formulate plans, and the United States sent advisers to evaluate and boost farm production. For the development of industry, which needed managerial talent, leading young businessmen were invited to New Delhi to discuss the strategy for advancing an indigenous technology.

The diversity of languages and the demand for linguistic provinces were a cause of large-scale riots. The

Parliamentary Committee, of which Indira was a member, conceded the demand for the creation of a Punjabi-speaking state. This led to demonstrations by the Hindus, and the violence spread to New Delhi, where a Hindu mob surrounded the main Sikh temple and threatened to sack it. Sikh guards drew their swords and charged into the unarmed mob. Finally the government ordered the police to suppress the rioting. Indira went to the Sikh temple area. In addressing a meeting, she condemned those responsible for the uprising. "There are no tears in my eyes," she said. "There is anger in my heart. Is it for disharmony that so many freedom fighters have sacrificed so much?"

In the northeast corner of India there was another kind of trouble. The Nagas and the Mizos living in the borderlands between India, Pakistan, and Burma were demanding an independent state of their own. The territory they held was in an inaccessible mountainous area. Pakistan supplied arms and trained the people in guerrilla warfare. The rebels indulged in terrorist activities, bombed trains, and disrupted communication between Assam and the rest of the country.

Indira ordered the air force to bomb concentrations of rebels and put down the rebellion. She went to Assam to discuss a settlement with the governor of the state, and this led to talks with representatives of the rebels. But incitement by Pakistan and China continued, and there was no settlement.

Some members of the Congress Working Committee and the Syndicate had supported Indira's candidacy in the January election because they felt that she would be amenable to their political designs, but they found out that she had a mind of her own. She was determined to project herself as a national leader. Lacking a hold on the party, she relied on her popularity with the masses. However, she had not yet achieved the position of indisputable leader held by Jawahar.

The party continued to hamper her, and at the same time the new opposition parties attempted to discredit the Congress party.

At the May, 1966, Congress party meeting, members criticized her for her food policy, which they considered too dependent on imports. Some contended that foreign aid undermines the nation's will to help itself. They attacked her for being subservient to the United States. There was a call for self-reliance as a substitute for massive foreign aid.

Indira was also attacked for having agreed to a proposed Indo-American Foundation for educational purposes. Congress party members alleged that such an establishment would be a cover for Central Intelligence Agency activities. When they further attacked her for abandoning her father's policy of nonalignment, she lashed out at her critics. Her father's foreign policy, she said, was flexible when circumstances required it. She climaxed her speech with a challenge:

"If you disapprove of my approach, then change your leadership. Remove me."

A dead silence. The critics did not accept the challenge. The press acclaimed her attitude, calling it "a return of the Nehru spirit."

A tidal wave of criticism of Indira's policies came in June, with the public announcement that the Indian rupee was devalued by 36 percent. Raja and I were in

New York when we heard the news on the radio. We knew that for years the World Bank had been pressing India to devalue her currency and that successive Finance Ministers had resisted the pressure. Raja was upset, and he phoned my cousin Bijju Nehru in Washington. Bijju said that he had cabled Indira his congratulations for a courageous decision. The problem, he said, was "no devaluation, no aid." Raja pointed out that a country like India, where 80 percent of exports consist of raw materials, cannot increase exports to earn more foreign exchange and improve her balance of trade.

In India the announcement was met with an uproar. The Congress President and other leaders criticized Indira openly. Indira, of course, had acted on the best advice available.

The summer months furnished her detractors with more grounds for attack. Food shortages, brought on by yet another monsoon poor in rain, led again to widespread riots. Strikers protested the rampant inflation and the consequent cost-of-living increases. Economic development came to a halt. Student agitation was commonplace. Opposition parties incited people to break laws and then demanded judicial inquiries on police action. From Communists to rightist reactionaries, all opposition parties had one aim: to discredit the Congress party and thereby defeat it in the 1967 elections. In turn, the Congress party deliberations took place against a backdrop of angry scenes. People lost confidence in the administration. Indira, however, did not lose courage or her faith in our people. She continued to put the interest of the country above all else.

Strikes called by both factory and government em-

ployees, to protest food shortages, low wages, and unsatis-
factory living standards, increased in intensity. There
were violent demonstrations against industrial manage-
ments and shop owners who refused to abide by *bandhs*
(forced closing of commercial and industrial establish-
ments).

Over the years, educational standards had deteriorated
in India. Now, in this period of unrest, students made
demands for lower fees, easier examinations, and the
granting of degrees even to those who had low scholastic
grades. Universities and colleges were overcrowded with
students who had no motivation for study; their only
motivation was to get a passport to jobs. Teacher-student
contacts hardly existed.

India's population explosion added to the need for increasing imports of food. At the same time there was a rise
in the cost of imported food grains, which tended to increase consumer prices and caused more discontent. The
population growth was due not so much to failure in the
practice of planned parenthood (Indian people do not
have the religious prejudices of a Christian society on the
question of contraception) but rather to advances in medical science. The government's health programs and improved medical facilities had resulted in a reduction of
both adult and infant death rates. The normal life ex-
pectancy had gone up from twenty-seven years to forty-
five.

One of India's most serious problems was the cow population, consisting of about 230 million useless cows. In
primitive Aryan societies, the dairy became the temple of
worship, and perhaps that is how cows became sacred in
the old Hindu society and were protected. In any agricul-

ture-oriented country, milch cattle are essential to the economy of the nation. But useless "sacred" cows eat up food that could sustain millions of hungry families.

The Jan Sangh, a chauvinist party of Hindu bigotry, started a campaign for the prohibition of cow slaughter. The motive of its members was the desire to strike at the central government, and therefore they did not take up their demands in the states, which alone had the constitutional powers for agricultural legislation. Having called on the government of India to prohibit cow slaughter, the Jan Sangh chose Delhi for demonstrations.

Thousands of *sadhus*—so-called holy men, most of whom are ignorant mendicants living on the credulity of the masses—were brought to Delhi by the Jan Sangh to demonstrate in front of the Parliament House, where the Lok Sabha was in session. Unfortunately, Gulzarilal Nanda, the Home Minister in charge of law and order, was a believer in the holiness of these illiterate men. He had accepted the presidency of the Sadhu Sangh (an association of *sadhus*). He had faith in their avowed professions of peace and took no steps to prevent their violent demonstration.

On November 7 a mob of half-naked, yelling *sadhus* carrying tridents, axes, and knives burned down cars and goverment buildings and assaulted individuals. Some threatened Congress President Kamaraj, who barely escaped. One minister's house was burned down. Belatedly, Nanda called in the police, but they were unable to stop the destruction of valuable government property and records.

Indira, who had just returned from a tour of the drought-stricken area of Bihar, addressed the Lok Sabha. "This is not an attack on the government," she said. "It is an attack on our way of life." She promised that henceforth violence would be put down with force. The Congress party demanded the removal of Home Minister Nanda. The party bosses had for a long time been trying to dominate Indira, and now they demanded a reshuffle of the Cabinet. She had planned to drop certain other ministers who had been forced on her when she became Prime Minister, but she succeeded only partially. Nanda was replaced by Chavan, but she was unable to drop two others whom she wanted to dismiss.

At this moment there was a deepening lack of confidence in her. It was even said that she would be dropped by the party. "She is nice, but she won't do," said one member of Parliament. And Kamaraj was reported to have said, "A big man's daughter, little man's big mistake." His little-man reference was to himself for having been Indira's erstwhile supporter. Newspaper comments, too, were adverse. The *sadhu* show of violence induced Frank Moraes, editor of the *Indian Express*, to write: "A prolonged policy of drift has ended in a disaster."

Under Communist influence, students from all over India planned a march on Parliament on November 18. However, the day passed quietly, because Chavan, the new Home Minister, had mobilized massive resources of police and armed forces to meet the threat.

The Jan Sangh, having failed with the *sadhus*, turned to other means. They brought Jagatguru Shankaracharya (from Puri in Orissa) to Delhi to begin his fast unto death for the purpose of persuading the government to enact legislation banning cow slaughter. The *jagatguru* (meaning "world teacher") claims to enjoy the same position for Hindus as the Pope does for Roman Catholics, though

there are, I believe, four *jagatgurus*. As the fast began,
large crowds came to obtain his *darshan* (blessing).
Anxiety about a possible riot caused the government to
order his arrest under preventive detention. He was removed to Pondicherry and kept there as a government
guest. In the end, his followers persuaded him to give up
the fast. These stunts were to cost the Jan Sangh a loss of
votes among decent people.

The threat of famine due to droughts remained the
most urgent problem. There was a lag in food shipments
from the United States—possibly because India had been
calling for a halt in the bombing of North Vietnam. Indira
turned to Australia, Canada, and France for the purchase
of food grains. And at home she entreated all parties to
join the government in helping to save people from starvation.

The year 1966 was plainly a crucial one in the economic
and political development of India. Indira was charting a
course to speed up the improvement of the Indian economy. She had many critics, but she was still a Nehru, with
personal appeal. As an effective vote-getter, there was no
one within the Congress party with her appeal.

24

The 1967 Elections

LIKE HER FATHER, Indira believed not only in gradual socialism for economic and social reforms but also in free enterprise. Her policies were in agreement with the goal of the Indian National Congress—namely, "a socialist state based on parliamentary democracy." Nevertheless, Krishna Menon attacked her in April, 1966, for allowing, he said, "a dangerous drift away from her father's policies."

Domestically, Indira sought to follow Gandhiji's ideals for the abolition of poverty. In foreign affairs, she tried to continue Jawahar's policy of independence and nonalignment. In October, 1966, Presidents Tito of Yugoslavia and Nasser of the United Arab Republic held talks with Indira in New Delhi. They called for an unconditional halt in the United States bombing of North Vietnam. This and Indira's previous denunciations of the bombing resulted in strained Indo-American relations. Nevertheless, United States food aid to India continued, though it was delayed and halting.

On the whole, 1966 was an unhappy year for India. Troubles were formidable: a second failure of the monsoon; riots over food shortages, especially in Kerala and West Bengal, and, toward the end of the year, in Bihar, Uttar Pradesh, and Madhya Pradesh; demonstrations and destruction of public property by students; the disgraceful spectacle of the *sadhus* rioting at the gates of Parliament House; violent language riots in Madras, the Punjab State, and New Delhi; a decline in agricultural production, an industrial slump, and a slowdown in economic growth; a sharp drop in foreign-exchange reserves; the formulation of a new five-year plan that projected nonachievable goals; antagonism to the devaluation of the rupee from 21 cents to 13.3 cents; inflation and the rise in prices of consumer goods; and the revolt of the tribesmen in the Naga and Mizo Hills of Assam.

In some respects, India's situation had counterparts elsewhere. Indira commented on similarities: "Which country in the world today is free from turmoil and internal strife? The United States with its race riots, student demonstrations, and violence? Japan with her student riots? The United Kingdom with its beatniks and labor strikes? We have come to a transition stage in our development when we must make one big effort to get over the hump."

But India's political leaders fell far short of making such an effort. The internal troubles had provided ammunition to dissident members of the Congress party who had expected Indira to be indecisive and pliant to their demands. Instead, she went her own way, intent on modernizing India. However, her lack of a personal following within the Congress party was detrimental to her relations with its leaders. She had bitter critics, who objected to her choice of advisers. While the country's economy was drifting to a standstill in the midst of widespread corruption and nepotism, the members of the Congress party seemed to be solely concerned with personal power and advancement. They wrangled about a choice of candidates for the March, 1967, election. Disgruntled factions existed in the central government and in the states. They were the old guard conservative elements; they wanted candidates who would be amenable to their dictates.

The Congress party had ruled the country for twenty years. In more recent years, discontent with its monolithic rule and pursuit of power began to spread. The administration was corrupt and ministers and high officials sought high positions in commerce and industry for their sons and other relatives in return for carrying out their official duties. A general unrest pervaded the Indian society. It produced a wave of new parties.

The opposition parties had a field day. They unleashed their desires to thwart the Congress party and capture power. They ranged from ultra-left Communists to reactionary rightists. One faction of Communists owed allegiance to Moscow, another to China. The socialists also comprised two factions.

There were two rightist parties, but of disparate aims. The Jan Sangh was the obscurantist party of Hindu reaction; it had incited the November 7 riots of *sadhus* in New Delhi. The Swatantra party consisted mainly of big-business conservative elements; it favored alliances with Western powers and therefore found some approval in the United States.

The Swatantra was formed in 1959 by Rajagopala- chari, who had once been a Congress leader and, later, Chief Minister of Madras. He had become a bitter critic of his erstwhile colleagues. (He was now ninety years old; unfortunately, in India no one likes to retire, even when reaching a ripe old age.) The Swatantra membership in- cluded former civil servants who, having collaborated with the British before India's independence, had been retained in civil service for their supposed "experience" to maintain administrative stability. On retirement from the service they had become "contact men" for foreign busi- ness. They re-entered politics to condemn the Congress, which had pampered them. They were the new "patri- ots."

The princes of the Indian states flocked to the Swa- tantra because the Congress party, after independence, had reduced their income to a mere percentage of the revenues of their states, whereas they formerly collected all the revenues. They had unlimited influence on voters, because in the Hindu way of life the ruler is the supreme "Father on Earth," who exacts and gets obedience.

There were other splinter parties. The Dravida Mun- netra Kazhaghan (DMK) functioned only in the South, in Madras State. It sought a separate autonomous state of Dravidians, who were the pre-Aryan residents of India, and it demanded that Hindustani should not be made the common language of India. This demand was supported by Rajagopalachari, even though he himself had intro- duced Hindustani in the Madras schools. Another DMK demand was that English should be retained as the official link language among the states, which was contrary to the constitution.

The February, 1967, general elections for the Lok Sabha and the state governments were to reveal the country's disenchantment with all parties. The opposition parties, having neither organization nor policies to attract voters, indulged in rowdyism and attempts to break up Congress meetings. Congress ministers were hurt; their cars were overturned and burned.

Indira's energetic campaigning belied those who had judged her as too frail for the burdens of a Prime Minister. Her grass-roots contacts in the villages and whistle-stop appearances in swings across the country made her feel secure in the love of the people. She attracted large crowds to her meetings.

At a turbulent meeting addressed by Indira in Bhuvaneshwar in Orissa, where the Swatantra hoped to win a majority of seats in the state government, stones were hurled. A brick hit Indira on the face, fracturing her nose. Security guards requested her to leave the rostrum, and congressmen begged her to take a seat at the back of the rostrum. Undaunted, holding a bloodied handkerchief against her nose, she faced the angry crowd. "This is an insult not to myself," she said, "but to the country, because as the Prime Minister of India I represent the country." The attack shocked the nation. All parties, at least publicly, condemned it. It was to cost the opposition parties many votes.

Indira's next stop was in a Communist stronghold in Calcutta, where she urged her audience to vote for Congress party candidates, reminding them that the Communists had not only thwarted the struggle for freedom in the "Quit India" movement but also sided with the enemy in the 1962 Chinese aggression.

On her return to Delhi, she found that the injury to her nose necessitated an operation. As usual, I was worried. When she was back home from the hospital, I phoned her long distance. In a mood of playful gravity, she said, "I am most upset. As soon as I came out of the anesthesia, I asked the doctor if he had done any plastic surgery and given me a beautiful nose. You know it it is too long and here was a chance to give me a beautiful nose, but the doctors failed to take the opportunity to improve my looks."

A few days before the Orissa episode, Indira had addressed a mammoth meeting at Jaipur, where a small group of noisy, jeering hecklers shouted for the ban on cow slaughter that had been promoted by the Jan Sangh. Her government had firmly refused to take this action, which would have harmed the national economy. Indira lost her famous temper as her voice rang out above the raucous catcalls.

"I am not going to be cowed down," she said. "I know who is behind these demonstrations, and I know how to make myself heard. I am going to do some plain speaking today. Your slogans do not change your past history. What were the Jan Sangh adherents doing when the country was under foreign rule? Go ask your maharaja and maharani how many wells they dug for their people, how many roads they constructed while they lived in luxury at the cost of the people. If you the people will only look at their achievements when they were your rulers, you will find a big zero." She spoke for an hour. The heckler's gibes were no longer heard. Everybody was listening.

Indira campaigned all over the country for candidates for the legislatures. She also, for the first time, had to go to the people for votes in the campaign for her own election in her own constituency. The voters of Phulpur (it had been Jawahar's constituency) invited her to be their candidate, but she decided to stand for election in Bareilly, which had been Feroze's constituency.

The February election results clearly showed that the Congress leaders were paying a penalty for their quarrels and reckless political games. Though the people of India still had regard for the Congress party, their votes indicated a lessened confidence in it. In the Lok Sabha, the party retained a majority, but the majority dropped from 70 percent to only 55 percent. The Syndicate leaders, who had tried to dominate the Congress party and Indira, were all defeated. Most meaningful was the defeat of Congress Party President Kamaraj by an unknown student in Madras State.

Opposition parties gained seats in the Lok Sabha. In nine of the seventeen states that held elections, the Congress party lost its majority; in eight states, the party retained power with a reduced majority. But the Congress party remained the biggest single party in every state except Madras and Kerala. Except for these two states, the opposition parties did not make large enough gains to form governments.

The state elections produced some coalition governments of strangely mixed elements (such as Communists and the Jan Sangh). In Kerala and West Bengal, the coalition governments were predominantly pro-Communist. In Madras, the predominant party was the DMK; in Orissa, the Swatantra party. Bihar and Punjab also had coalition governments.

Indira, having won with a huge majority, was now established as the national leader. Morarji Desai also won with a large majority. When I expressed my anxiety about the future of relations between the states and the central government, Indira made a laconic comment:

"I am proud of our democracy. If the people wish to choose other than a Congress nominee, they should do so. It is their right to choose whomever they wish, just as it is their right to choose the Prime Minister."

25

Tackling Enormous Economic and Political Problems

IMMEDIATELY AFTER the election results were announced, the leaders—Kamaraj, Patil, and others—rushed to New Delhi for a meeting of the Congress Working Committee and the Parlimentary Board. As far as the party in Parliament was concerned, the obvious choice for Prime Minister was Indira, but Morarji Desai, who had contested against her in 1966, was preparing to contest her selection by the party once again. The reverses the Congress party had suffered in the elections pointed to the necessity of a unanimous choice if the party was to maintain its unity and regain its former position in the country. With a slender majority in the Parliament, it was all the more necessary to avoid internal struggle for power, which could weaken the government and threaten the very existence of the Congress rule. Indira desired a unanimous choice, but she was prepared to face a contest if it came. Morarji Desai was a loyal and disciplined party member, but he was not prepared to give up his claim to the leadership of the party unless he was given an important position in the new government. Indira on the other hand was not prepared to give up her unfettered right to choose her own Cabinet. And so once again the contest between the two seemed inevitable.

At the last moment a compromise was arrived at between the two claimants for the leadership, and on March 12, Indira was elected unanimously as the Prime Minister and Morarji Desai became the Deputy Prime Minister.

The unanimity of the choice can be understood, for no other possible candidate had Indira's experience in statesmanship, her appeal to the masses, and the strength of her personality. As long ago as March, 1964, Nan (several times Indian ambassador to foreign countries) had said, "Indira has risen by sheer value of her worth, and the work she has done. . . . It's absolutely in the fitness of things that she has reached the position she has today."[1] This comment was even more relevant in 1967.

Indira proceeded to form her government. She retained some of the old members of the Cabinet and brought in a few young members. On May 9, through her influence, a Muslim, Dr. Zakir Hussain, was elected President of India.

Some of the problems of 1966 continued to trouble India: the old dispute with Pakistan over Kashmir; public disaffection with the Congress party leadership; violence over food deficits and linguistic and religious issues; criticism of the foreign policy; the call for India's self-help in place of foreign aid; the lack of implementation of the April, 1966, five-year plan; inflation and the cost-of-living rise; and the strained state of the national economy. And

tacked on to this stress of circumstances was the in-
tractableness of the recently formed state coalition governments, with central and state leaders operating at cross
purposes.

New problems arose. In drought-plagued Bihar, drink-
ing water and fodder for cattle dried up in a disastrous
water shortage that added thirst to hunger. An eye witness said, "Thirst is more degrading than hunger." Indira
appealed to the people to make greater efforts to help
themselves. She asked foreign governments for help, and
the government succeeded in saving millions of lives.

Trouble with China developed in September on the
Tibet frontier. There were Chinese-Indian confrontations
of troops at the Himalayan border. Demonstrators rioted
at the Chinese Embassy in New Delhi and the Indian
Embassy in Peking.

In June war broke out in the Middle East, and Indira's
pro-Arab policy came under much criticism both at home
and abroad. That criticism, I believe, failed to consider
India's national interests. Indira's attitude was not based
on religion, race, or nationality. She is deeply conscious of
the inhuman persecution of the Jewish people in World
War II, which she had herself witnessed in Europe. She is
also conscious of Arab suffering under colonialism and
imperialism. Besides, Jews and Arabs are historically the
same people; they have lived side by side for centuries.
Indira continues to follow the policy that was formulated
by Jawahar: nonalignment, but not neutrality. India seeks
to judge the merits of each issue through enlightened self-
interest—enlightened by the moral values we hold.

We are not anti-Jewish in any way, but with a large
number of religious minorities within our country, our

very existence as a stable democracy depends upon secularism within and around us. On our western and eastern frontiers there are forces of religious intolerance which seek to unify the Islamic nations against us. It is therefore necessary for us to support those who work for secularism.

In July the monsoon came, and with it plentiful rain and a promise of better harvests. Our parched and hungry land was turned into smiling green fields.

Meanwhile, the power crazy politicians in many state legislatures changed and rechanged their party affiliations in a search for high offices, and ministries changed hands every few days. The instability of administration disrupted the economic revival, while strikes and *Bandhs* fomented by parties in power created an utter sense of despair in the country.

Programs of national development got underway. Under Indira's guidance, plans were pushed forward to make the country self-sufficient in food. The budget for agricultural development was increased by large amounts. Large quantities of fertilizers were distributed, and the farmers were advised on their proper use. The United States made grain available through the Food for Peace program and sent technical-aid teams to train Indians in techniques of farming and marketing. Improvement in agricultural technology was given top priority. New high-yielding varieties of grain were produced, and crops rose above previous records. As food scarcity lessened hopes of economic development rose.

The image of the Congress party, which had been tarnished by the altercations among its leaders and the neglect of governmental needs, had to be improved;

harmony between central and state governments had to be fostered; the confidence of the people had to be restored. This would take time.

The first fourteen months of Indira's administration had been characterized as a "caretaker," or pro-tem, government, because she had not been put in office through a general election. The 1967 general election had rejected the party bosses and given the people's support to her. Now her authority was strengthened, and she had a full five years to initiate and carry out her policies.

For her people—for the place India would hold in the comity of nations—she looked to the decades ahead: "The next ten or twelve years will be only the first milestone. But within the time-span of the next decade or so, India, we believe and we pray, will emerge as a fully self-reliant nation."[2]

26

"*Let My Country Awake*"

WHAT IS INDIRA LIKE as a person? What is she like as a mother? Does she, and will she, make the kind of Prime Minister India needs? Much has been written about her, yet these questions continue to be asked of me. It is difficult for me to answer them because to me she is everything I had hoped of the girl I had watched and looked after as she grew up. I have loved her too much to find any shortcomings in her. What then can I say of her except that she is a true daughter of our family? The people of India have loved our family, and they give Indira their abundant affection.

Indira is a beautiful woman, and everything around her —in the home environment—is also beautiful. Though overburdened with work, she takes time for housewifely duties—seeing to the daily menus, the orderliness of her home, and the training and welfare of her servants. She has a gift for making attractive flower arrangements. Her clothes are chosen with taste. In her lovely saris and elegant Kashmiri shawls, she is exquisitely feminine. A Washington reporter, surprised to hear that a visiting head of state had gone to a hairdresser before the state banquet with which President Johnson honored her in 1966, said, "But she is feminine." What did he expect her to be?

She is a woman and proud of being one. We are not bluestockings, nor are we feminists. We are happy to do whatever job we are called upon to do, and our home and children are a big part of our job. Indira's two sons have always been her first concern. While they were away studying in England, she wrote them regularly and spent much time with them on her trips to London. Rajiv went to Cambridge, to the college attended by his grandfather Jawahar, but Sanjay preferred a practical rather than a college education. He had a few years of apprenticeship in one of England's automobile manufactories. Both sons are now at home, to their mother's delight. They are handsome and companionable young men and deeply affectionate. The house is once again filled with their voices and three jubilant golden retrievers.

Indira did not encourage her sons to enter politics, nor did they want to. She told an interviewer that she wished them to make a contribution to industry. "Technology, you know, is very important to our development."[1]

I had hoped that my elder son, Harsha, would go into politics and keep the tradition of our family alive, but he did not have the desire to do so. I often wonder whether the name of Nehru will fade away into the pages of our country's history, or whether there will be some future Nehru still doing his or her bit for the new and resurgent India.

There are those who describe Indira as cold, aloof, arrogant, snobbish. Actually, she is warm and friendly. The shyness of her childhood days, stemming from loneliness, still persists with strangers, and this might make her seem aloof. Some foreign writers have ascribed the supposed arrogance of the Nehru clan to our being Brahmins. A Brahmana is a teacher, a man of knowledge. He is "twice born," because at the age of nine or ten, when he puts on the sacred thread, he receives "grace" and goes to a guru in search of knowledge. A man of knowledge has humility and deep humanism; he is only an aristocrat of intellect, not of birth or privilege. If this is the implication of those foreign writers, then I am grateful that we are Brahmin aristocrats.

Once, during World War I, I went to the Haffekine Institute to donate blood to its blood bank. The head of the institute—General Sokhey, a physician devoted to medical research—was a friend of the family. He jokingly remarked, "Sorry Krishna, your blood is not blue; it is just common red." I replied, "What do you think? I am just a Brahmin."

Throughout Indira's childhood and adolescence, Jawahar had tried, by means of his letters from prison, to instill in her a reverence for the values and ideals transmitted by the history of mankind. Those lessons became a part of her being. After she had assumed the office of Prime Minister, an interviewer questioned her about the values and ideals that inspire the people of India today. She said:

These values and ideals are born out of a synthesis of the old and new in our history and our life. Take our old spirit of tolerance and the universal view. It is, perhaps, out of this that the new concept of peaceful coexistence has grown. Then there is the new awareness of the people's right to a better life—not only material but also cultural and intellectual life—and this awareness gets concretised in the "socialistic pattern of society" that we are pledged to create for our people. Again, that awareness gets extended to our foreign policy, which is based on the simple idea that we want for others, too, the values of peace and freedom and an opportunity for progress that we want for ourselves.[2]

When Indira first became Prime Minister, she faced a responsibility far heavier than either her father or Lal Bahadur Shastri had to face. The country was in the grip of famine, inflation, and an increasing cost of living, for which an impatient people, in their lack of understanding, blamed the government. An irresponsible opposition saw an opportunity for capturing power and incited the people to disrupt law and order. An India that had known stability and orderly progress for eighteen years was sunk into disorder and disruption. In spite of the years of training Indira had, she was new and somewhat halting when the responsibility of guiding the country was placed in her hands. Entering the Parliament for the first time, she was inexperienced in parliamentary procedures. But by now she is on firmer ground and handles her Cabinet and the Parliament with the skill of an old parliamentarian. In the words of a Cabinet member who had been a minister under the previous two Prime Ministers, "In clarity, brevity of expression, taking decisions with the courage of conviction, and the forthright manner in stating what she feels, she has excelled her two illustrious predecessors."[3]

We are a people of common clay, with weaknesses and strengths. Indira may be, as critics have said, weak in some ways, but she has courage and determination. In her veins flows the blood of her father and grandfather, who were dedicated to the cause of India, to the great ideals which have grown out of the long history of our land. Indira was born in Allahabad, the ancient sacred city of Prayag, on the broad bosom of the Ganga—the river of India round which "are entwined her [India's] racial memories, her hopes and fears, her songs of triumph, her victories and defeats." This, then, is Indira's heritage. Like the Ganga, she belongs to India, and India is the one passion of her life—our India, our people. As long as she lives, she will devote herself to keeping the promises made by Jawahar:

"I do dedicate myself in all humility to the service of India and her people to the end that this ancient land attain her rightful place in the world and make her full and willing contribution to the promotion of world peace and the welfare of mankind."

This is the vision of India that inspired Jawahar:

Where the mind is without fear and the head is held high;
Where knowledge is free;
Where the world has not been broken up into fragments by narrow domestic walls;
Where words come out from the depth of truth;
Where tireless striving stretches its arms towards perfection;
Where the clear stream of reason has not lost its way into the dreary desert sand of dead habit;

Where the mind is led forward by thee into ever-widening thought and action—
Into that heaven of freedom, my Father, let my country awake.

—TAGORE, *Gitanjali*

Notes

Chapter 3
1. Jawaharlal Nehru, *Toward Freedom* (New York: John Day Co., 1942), p. 48.

Chapter 4
1. J. Nehru, *op. cit.*, p. 69.
2. Arnold Michaelis, "An Interview with Indira Gandhi," *McCall's*, April, 1966, p. 191.
3. Krishna Nehru Hutheesing, *We Nehrus* (New York: Holt, Rinehart & Winston, 1967), p. 55.

Chapter 5
1. J. Nehru, *op. cit.*, p. 230.
2. B. R. Nanda, *The Nehrus* (New York: John Day Co., 1963), p. 293.
3. K. N. Hutheesing, *op. cit.*, pp. 81–82.
4. J. Nehru, *op. cit.*, pp. 388–89.
5. B. R. Nanda, *op. cit.*
6. Arnold Michaelis, *op. cit.*, p. 188.
7. J. Nehru, *op. cit.*
8. J. Nehru, *Glimpses of World History* (New York: John Day Co., 1942), p. 54. First published in England in two volumes, 1934.

Chapter 6

1. J. Nehru, *Glimpses of World History*, p. 6.
2. *Ibid.*, pp. 1–3.
3. *Ibid.*, pp. 4–5.
4. J. Nehru, *Toward Freedom*, p. 237.
5. J. Nehru, *Glimpses of World History*, pp. 949-53.
6. Krishna Nehru, *With No Regrets* (New York: John Day Co., 1945), pp. 98–99.
7. J. Nehru, *Toward Freedom*, p. 298.
8. K. N. Hutheesing, *We Nehrus*, p. 139.

Chapter 7

1. J. Nehru, *Toward Freedom*, p. 338.
2. J. Nehru, *The Discovery of India* (New York: John Day Co., 1946), pp. 27–32 *passim*.
3. *Ibid.*, p. 36.
4. *Ibid.*

Chapter 8

1. J. Nehru, *A Bunch of Old Letters* (Bombay: Asia Publishing House, 1958).
2. Mohammed Yunus, *Frontier Speaks*.
3. J. Nehru, *Glimpses of World History*, pp. 954 and 956.
4. J. Nehru, *A Bunch of Old Letters*, p. 408.

Chapter 10

1. Arnold Michaelis, *op. cit.*, p. 188.
2. Vijaya Lakshmi Pandit, *Prison Days*.

Chapter 12

1. K. N. Hutheesing, *We Nehrus*, p. 176.

Chapter 14

1. *Nehru on Gandhi: A Selection from the Writings and Speeches of Jawaharlal Nehru* (New York: John Day Co., 1948) pp. 141 and 146.

Chapter 15

1. K. N. Hutheesing, *We Nehrus*, p. 237.

2. *Ibid.*
3. Dorothy Norman (ed.), *Nehru: The First Sixty Years* (New York: John Day Co., 1965), Vol. II, p. 98.

Chapter 16

1. Betty Friedan, "How Mrs. Gandhi Shattered 'The Feminine Mystique,'" *Ladies Home Journal*, May, 1966, p. 165.
2. *Ibid.*

Chapter 19

1. Dorothy Norman, *op. cit.*, pp. 574 and 575.
2. *Ibid.*, p. 573.

Chapter 20

1. K. N. Hutheesing, *We Nehrus*, p. 306.

Chapter 22

1. J. Nehru, *The Discovery of India*, p. 109.
2. *Ibid.*, pp. 239–40.
3. William Attwood, "A Frank Talk with a Powerful Woman," *Look*, April 30, 1968, p. 82.

Chapter 25

1. Arnold Michaelis, *op. cit.*, p. 105.
2. Robert Hardy Andrews, *A Lamp for India* (Englewood Cliffs, N. J., Prentice-Hall, 1967), p. 388.

Chapter 26

1. Arnold Michaelis, *op. cit.*, p. 105.
2. K. A. Abbas, *Indira Gandhi* (Bombay: Popular Prakashan, 1966).
3. *Ibid.*

Index

92 ♂   11964

DATE DUE

JAN 3 1 1974			
MAR 2 6 1996			

92
♂
C 1

Hutheesing, Krishna Nehru
Dear to behold

B 30-276